# LOVE
## AND
# SELLING

# LOVE
## AND
# SELLING

*Suck less at selling*

## Dan Smaida

BEAVER'S
POND
PRESS

I have tried to recreate events, locales, and conversations from my memories of them. In order to maintain their anonymity in some instances I have changed the names of individuals and places, I may have changed some identifying characteristics and details such as physical properties, occupations, and places of residence.

Although the author and publisher have made every effort to ensure that the information in this book was correct at press time, the author and publisher do not assume and hereby disclaim any liability to any party for any loss, damage, or disruption caused by errors or omissions, whether such errors or omissions result from negligence, accident, or any other cause.

ISBN 13: 978-1-59298-644-6

Library of Congress Catalog Number: 2015918944

Printed in the United States of America
First Printing: 2016
20   19   18   17   16      5   4   3   2   1

Cover and interior design by James Monroe Design, LLC.

BEAVER'S
POND
PRESS

Beaver's Pond Press, Inc.
7108 Ohms Lane
Edina, MN  55439–2129
(952) 829-8818
www.BeaversPondPress.com

To order, visit www.realrelationshipselling.com

Booksellers visit www.ItascaBooks.com
or call (800)-901-3480. Reseller discounts available.

*For everyone who has loved me and shown me how to love,*
*you made this book possible. Thank you.*

*Love is both a goal and a journey.*
*Pursue what you love, and love the pursuit.*

# This Book Is for You If . . .

. . . you sell for a living and are proud of it.

. . . you sell solutions that involve more than just products.

. . . you must assess and develop needs, not just meet them. In other words, you're in sales, not customer service.

. . . you need to develop relationships, not just conduct transactions.

. . . you rely on visual, vocal, and verbal communication to make sales. In other words, you're a human, not a computer.

. . . you compete for business against similar offers. In other words, you work in business, not government.

. . . you sell to customers with complex, sometimes obtuse decision-making structures and processes.

. . . you reject traditional thinking that tries to turn selling into a box-checking exercise.

. . . you look with suspicion at any self-styled sales guru who tries to sell you a guaranteed process or foolproof system.

. . . you run away from sales managers who manage by numbers alone and measure you based on spurious activity metrics, like how many proposals you've sent this week.

. . . you take an interest in psychology, behavioral economics, and emotional intelligence.

. . . you work with a sense of purpose, not just to work.

. . . you care about your customers just as much as your commissions—and understand which comes first.

. . . you are willing to pony up the money for this book. In other words, you are not a pirate.

. . . you don't take yourself or your profession too seriously.

. . . you are not easily offended.

# Contents

# Why This Book Is Overdue

## It's Time to Stop the Cringing

In over twenty years of managing, training, and coaching salespeople, I've seen a lot of spectacular—and spectacularly bad—selling. It's my intolerance of the latter that brings us together today. Please let me explain.

When I first started paying attention to the difference between good and bad selling, it was funny. Oh, how I would laugh inwardly when a salesperson would show up, throw up, and get kicked out in short order. "Job security," I chuckled to myself. "I will always have work as a sales trainer." Just like I used to laugh into my Cheetos when *America's Funniest Home Videos* showed someone getting smacked in the testicles.

Well, I don't laugh at those crotch-smacking videos anymore, and I no longer secretly enjoy watching salespeople struggle. In fact, now I sort of feel bad about it—even a mild form of self-reproof, particularly when it's someone I know. After all, what kind of person laughs when their friend gets whacked in the onions?[1]

---

1.  Full disclosure: I am that kind of person. In fact, just writing these paragraphs made me LOL, as the kids say.

So I'm doing something about it. I shall attempt, through the Lens of Love, to reveal the limitations of traditional sales behaviors. In real life, if we tried some of the things we take for granted in selling, they would result in a slap, a restraining order . . . or a swift kick in the grapes.

I'll also show you alternatives to traditional, customary sales behaviors—how acting based on the principles of loving relationships helps create business results. If you believe, like I do, that caring about people is the foundation of good business, this book is for you.

It's time to stop the cringing.

## This Is Not Your Cheesy Uncle's Sales Book

I've been observing sales calls, coaching sales strategy, and conducting sales training workshops for the last twenty years or so. In that time, we've witnessed an explosion of sales thought, much of it in the form of business books that *appear* to be like this one.

Of course, this book has something in common with other books on selling. I'm attempting to impart a philosophy, outline a strategy, and share models and techniques that I've seen work over and over.[2] I say "appear to be like this one," though, because at the core, most sales books are either dancing at the edges of or missing the point altogether.

Most sales books are more about business relationships than human relationships. As such, they focus mostly on the behaviors necessary to the business, not the people involved. And that's a tragedy, because human relationships are the fundamental core of business relationships. This book is about how people relate to

---

2.    I would also be okay with selling a few copies.

people—selling is just an application. My fondest wish is that you apply the principles of this book to your whole life, not just your business life.

Most sales books focus on the *process* of sellers getting what they want. That's why you see a lot of artificial processes and models that attempt to turn selling into a recipe. Even if you have the customer's best interests at heart, using a seller-centered process can work against you. This book is about ditching the seller-centeredness and focusing on the relationship you're trying to create—it's about relating.

Most sales books focus almost exclusively on the how-to— they're full of advice and action steps you're supposed to follow. But in reality, we often get more value from how-not-to advice. A wise man once said, "The secret to a long life? Don't die young." This book is about avoiding some of the traps and pitfalls traditional how-to sales books often unwittingly encourage. Therefore, I will spend a lot of time in this book warning you about traps, pitfalls, and cow pies to step around.

## This Book Is Long Overdue

This book is long overdue because we need to break the seller-centric habit—following a sales "process" and forgetting the essential truth of business: it's about *people first and business second*. Be prepared to reexamine why you do some of the things you do.

This book is long overdue because I had the insight several years ago but spent a ton of time validating, developing, and refining the thesis in my work with clients. I've spent the last twenty years gathering the kind of empirical data you can't get with a psychology experiment on a bunch of graduate students, and that's taken a lot of time.

This book is long overdue because, having had the insight, I am now totally unable to watch poor selling happen—it's too uncomfortable. Consider this treatise part of my contribution to reducing the cringe factor in selling.

This book is long overdue because my clients have been asking me for it for several years. You're welcome. I'm sure I can count on you to buy a copy.

## This Book Is Not Trendy

This is an essay—not a scientific research paper, not a doctoral thesis, not a statistical analysis (which a lot of sales books today are trying to resemble). So you're not going to see a bunch of citations, laborious endnotes with fancy words like *ibid.* (which, until recently, I thought was a long-legged wading bird) and *op. cit.* (a polite way of saying, "I just told you that"). I will use very few statistics to support my arguments, thereby bucking the current trend of authors reaching for numbers that validate their positions (a trick called *selective evidence*) or trying to prop up a flimsy argument with a bunch of impressive-looking numbers (a trick called bulls—ing).

For an essay to be interesting, it should be debatable. And when you're talking about subjective things like love and selling, there will be plenty in this book you can debate. And you should—this book is meant to stimulate your thinking, ask you to reconsider some "conventional wisdom" in selling, and question your current beliefs and behaviors.

So I promise to keep the bulls—statistics to a minimum if you promise to actively question what you read and think about how it applies to you and your life. Deal? Deal.

## It's Easy to Argue with This Book

First, the principle of confirmation bias (covered more deeply in part 1) says that we tend to seek confirmatory evidence and block out contradictory evidence. So when I call out a cheesy sales behavior you've used your whole career, you may have one or more of these common reactions.

The most common reaction to my counterintuitive advice is, "Smaida doesn't understand my sale; my sale is different." And you're partly right—but even when I don't understand *your* sale, I understand *sales*. I will be speaking about generalities and universalities (which is really a word). And you'd be wise to consider these universalities if 2 + 2 = 4 everywhere else in the world. Is there a possibility that holds in your sale? Or is your sale truly subject to unique rules?

Those of you in an RFP (request for proposal) or tender-heavy (for my European friends) sale will react to this book by saying, "It's all about price. Procurement and the consultants have sucked all the relationship out of my sale."

To this argument, I have two thoughts. First, responding to an RFP is not selling. It's quoting. That's different. If your entire job consists of filling out RFP templates and doing presentations and you're getting paid like a salesperson, good for you! You've clearly made at least one sale—to your bosses.

Second thought: I've rarely seen an RFP process that didn't involve and revolve around relationships. Somebody (a person) built the relationship that led to the RFP, somebody (again, a person) helped the customer write it, and somebody has the inside track because that somebody has built better relationships.

Some of you will hear me caution against things you've been doing your whole career. Your reaction will be some form of "I've been quite successful doing it my way" (quota achiever, president's club, etc.). It's been written in the sour expressions on many a workshop participant of mine.

Well, congratulations on your success. But am I congratulating you on your effectiveness or on your luck? Let's face it: Salespeople have a lot less control of our fates than we'd like to believe. Plenty of salespeople have benefited from randomness and "right place, right time" circumstances that have little to do with effectiveness.

Example: In my first sales management job, I had an advertising sales rep who was sort of sitting around, minding his own business, when a major PC manufacturer called up out of the blue and placed a major series of giant ads. (This was back when print newspapers still freely roamed the earth.) This rep (let's call him Eric) went from good to extremely successful in the course of one phone call. I'm going to go out on a limb and suggest that Eric did not magically become more *effective* the moment this bluebird called. Eric simply became *luckier* in that moment. Later, Eric became *angrier* when I jacked his quota.

So argue if you must. I will take that as a sign that my attempts to be provocative are working. I look forward to your e-mail and your anonymous trashing on Amazon.com.

# *How to Use This Book*

As I write these words, one of the most popular forms of communication is Twitter. (Well, that and selfies.) As the average serving size of information has shrunk, so has our general familiarity with books. Nonfiction books[3] in particular—one common reaction to handing someone a business book is one of "Oh, I could never make it through all that. It's so dry."

Well, this may be dry as sawdust cupcakes with sand frosting, but that doesn't mean you have to suffer through the whole thing in sequence. This isn't a story; it's an essay with multiple facets, all of which examine the analogous relationship between love and selling.

So start anywhere you like (although I recommend the first twelve pages as a good launching point). Feel free to skip around. Find things you like in the table of contents and go there. And by all means, skip the boring parts. Life's too short.

I encourage you to use this book as a lens through which you examine and reexamine your everyday selling. If you become more introspective and reflective about the sales behaviors you use every day, my job is complete. When my skeptically raised eyebrow haunts your sales meeting preparation and review, then I have fulfilled my mission as a professional sales provocateur.

---

3. I sincerely hope you view this essay as a work of nonfiction.

Writing this book has been important to my own self-development. I use the Lens of Love more than ever in my relationships inside and outside of work. I am haunted by my own skeptically raised eyebrow. Hopefully I am a better husband, father, son, brother, cousin, and business partner because of it. Use this book to achieve the same gains in your life, and it will be worth the medium-low bucks you shelled out for it.

# PART
# ONE

*Love and Selling Are Analogous*

# What Is Love?

I n my opinion, *love* is one of those multipurpose words one can twist and jiggle to make a number of different points. First, there's the feeling you have for someone—you *love* them. There's also the state you find yourself in—you're *in love*. There's the physical act ("I wanna love you all over"). And, of course, there's love as an object ("the love of my life"). And there's the kind of love you make . . . good? Good.

In this book, I will mostly discuss the feeling of love (an emotional attachment) you're trying to create (or approximate) by using sound principles and effective behaviors. There just so happens to be a business transaction involved.

## How Do Love and Selling Relate?

When I say *love* in this book (and I will, over and over), I might be describing the concept (a loving relationship built on trust and vulnerability). I might be describing the feeling (you love something).

When I talk about the concept of love, I might use it as a metaphor ("Love is a battlefield"). I might use it as a simile ("Selling to prospects who can't buy is like looking for a dance partner in a morgue").

Most importantly, I use love as an *analogy*: I'll harp on how love and selling are similar in so many ways that they are parallel, and thus worth examining for lessons that can be taken from one and applied to the other. I just so happen to think the lessons of love are useful in business. (Also, I'm sure the equivalent to "how to sell someone on loving you" has already been written. Many times.)

That's so deep, I'm gonna say it again: Love and selling are similar in so many ways. Take a lesson from love and use it to be a better seller. The end. Thank you.

## Love Matters

So what's love got to do with it? Consider the following truths:

- People buy with emotion and justify with logic.

- People buy from people.

- You've bought things simply because you loved the people selling to you.

- You've walked away from things you need because the seller turned you off.

The point: underestimate the importance of human relationship at your own peril. Part of the value of this book is in helping you realize just how much love really matters. In my experience, you can't *overestimate* the impact of feelings, needs, and relationships. They *always* matter more than you think.

Along those lines. . .

## Love Is Higher Than a Mountain

Throughout history, people have done amazing things for love. In the Old Testament, Ruth forsook her family (and her inheritance) for love. Consider such examples of love as Menaelus and Helen of Troy (for whom he "launched a thousand ships" and began the Trojan War); Peter Abelard and Héloïse; Edward (Prince of Wales) and the American Mrs. Simpson (for whom he abdicated the throne). And that's before we even get to Romeo and Juliet.

In business, love is often thicker than water. When customers love their sellers, personal loyalty often trumps loyalty to a product or service. They justify emotional decisions with logic and data. They introduce you to the right people. They even put vendors through empty RFP processes where the decision has already been made . . . in their hearts.

Have you ever been told as a seller to work on "building walls around your customers"? Well, I have news for you—you can't. You can't prevent competitors from calling, you can't prevent customers from entertaining other options, and you can't stop them from leaving, even if you have a contract. Contracts end, and contracts get breached. (Just like you can't stop that jerk/harlot from hitting on your honey at the bar—the same way you can't stop your honey from dumping you for said jerk/harlot.)

But customers who love you? *They* build walls around your business. They don't take your competitors' calls, they don't entertain other options, and they don't care about contracts—they have a personal contract with you. Even if they are forced to entertain other options, loyal customers will give you inside information on how to win, help you from the inside, and give you the "last look"—an opportunity to save business at risk. It's like your honey giving that jerk/harlot the brushoff.

## Love Is All about Value

In my workshops, I encourage salespeople to define value simply as *worth*: is it worth it to pursue a particular course of action?

Have you ever known someone who stayed in what looked to you like a bad relationship? Or someone who left a seemingly great situation to run off with their personal assistant? Or someone who sports an extremely unfortunate tattoo? Even when it's not clear to the viewer, people are constantly guided, even driven, by their own internal value equation—their answer to "Is it worth it?" And what makes someone worth it in love is value: part *shared values* (you strive for the same things) and *value derived* (you get something particular out of the relationship).

Am I stretching the analogy to offer the metaphor that love is a value equation? Does that bother you? Well, now's your chance to put this book down and do something less uncomfortable—because analogy stretching is going to happen in this book. A lot.

## Looking through the Lens of Love

Throughout this book, we'll be looking through the *Lens of Love*. Through this lens, we'll compare business relationships to loving relationships. We'll look at whether conventional sales wisdom applies to building durable, loving relationships. We'll examine traditional sales behaviors through the Lens of Love and ask, "Would you really do this in love?"

Spoiler alert: When you look at sales through the Lens of Love, some of the stuff you do starts to look a little dumb. Many of the behaviors that pass for good selling would get you dumped in real life. Many of the things you would never do at home, you do all the time at work. You unintentionally suck a little bit at selling.

Looking through the Lens of Love adds a vital perspective to selling—the true relationship perspective. And in today's hyper-competitive business world, where product/service superiority is harder to achieve and sustain than ever, human relationships continue to matter. It's when sellers view their customers as objects of affection (rather than *with affection*) that a lot of the sucky selling starts.

If the Lens of Love doesn't make you reconsider some of your tried-and-true sales behaviors, I'll eat this whole box of Valentine's Day chocolates. I mean it.

# Salespeople Are Hired to Suck at Selling

*I must know immediately, before we proceed apace,*
*Will you buy from me?*
*Will you buy from me forever?*
*Let me ponder it overnight. Seller, seller, let me ruminate.*

*Let me slumber on it, and I'll give you an answer*
*ere the dawn.*

—SIR LOAF OF MEAT, SIXTEENTH-CENTURY SELLER/MINSTREL

## The Myth of the Extroverted Closer

When I started hiring and training salespeople twenty years ago, the profile was salespeople with "drive," "closers." "Go-getters" who are "aggressive." The motto was ABC: Always Be Closing.

Then the psychologists got involved and replaced those dinosaur words with more evolved, academic[4] terms like *extroversion*, *ego drive*, and *perseverance*. I have just worked with a client whose hiring profile included these very terms, and I see it consistently:

---

4.   And thus seemingly more valid.

sales organizations continue to lean toward the traditional extroverted sales profile.

The problem, as I see it: Many top-down hiring practices today involve executive involvement or sign-off on new sales hires (particularly in companies who boast of hiring "rigor"). Such senior leaders, by definition, enjoy both more tenure (read: "old school") and more distance from today's selling reality (read: "out of touch"). Often, this final say in hiring actually represents the old-school bias.

No doubt, some of these traditional sales qualities are useful some of the time. There are moments when a little extroversion can help overcome call reluctance, for instance. But it's a mistake to assume these qualities are *necessary* for success in selling. In fact, the overuse of these competencies is what gives selling a bad name.

Both of the young lovers in this sales version of the Meatloaf song, "Paradise by the Dashboard Light," express some of the very worst qualities of professional sellers. They're hyper-focused on closing the deal. Their sole concern is their own deadline—they "gotta know right now." They're ultra-persistent—no amount of objections will deter them from the goal. They're grabby. And in many cases, these qualities lead to deals that should never have been closed in the first place.

And that's the risk of having a sales force full of traditional sales types—deals get closed, but they're not all good ones. Deadlines get met, but at what costs? Agendas get pushed, but customers get pushed away. Salespeople, or sales forces, without balance tend to produce unintended consequences that hamper long-term results.

Let's face it—when confronted with Sir Loaf's aggressive approach, you probably would have called for an Uber.

## Missing the Important Stuff

Unfortunately, sellers with a high degree of extroversion, ego drive, and go-getter-ness often lack a sufficient degree of characteristics that are key to the high-level, consultative sale. In my experience as a coach for, consultant to, and leader of sales teams, these characteristics are underrated compared to the extroverted-closer traits.

The first underrated trait is *empathy*, which I'll define more closely later on. For now, think of it as the ability to identify with another. Are you picking up what they're putting down? Are you smelling what they're stepping in? Are you taking another's perspective?

With high degrees of go-getting often come a lack of *deliberation*—thoughtful consideration before acting based on reflection and forethought. It's the rare ABC salesperson who also possesses high degrees of deliberation. But deliberation is often highly necessary in a complex environment.

Finally, the action orientation of the hard-driving, aggressive closer often comes at the expense of *thoughtfulness* and *sensitivity*. Yes, salespeople need to be confident enough to ask for the business . . . *and* thoughtful and sensitive enough to know when it's not time or when closing could be considered premature or pushy.

Let's look at this through the Lens of Love. Do you want a partner who knows what they want, is not afraid to ask for it, and is willing to go for it? Of course you do. (Or maybe you don't—after all, this is love.) But if that person is also inconsiderate, thoughtless, and insensitive, you will have a fun time on the date but an ultimately cold and empty relationship.

## Viva the Ambivert!

In the book *Quiet*, Susan Cain examines how the qualities of the introvert are actually an advantage in more complex, extended sales cycles.

The yang to the extrovert's yin is the introvert. These folks get their energy from solitude and intimacy and tend to have to work at being in crowds, meeting new people, and dealing with noise. In other words, they have to work at being salespeople. If a day of meetings and presentations leaves you cooked and in need of quiet time to yourself, you may possess elements of the introvert.

So what makes introverts uniquely qualified to succeed in higher-level sales? Things like:

- listening deeply and not just waiting until it's their turn to talk

- responding to a customer's statement with deeper questions and not just opinions

- patiently processing and not rushing to judgment or jumping to conclusions

- relating to introvert customers with a pace, tone, and volume that create comfort

The more complex the sales environment, the more these competencies matter and the more they differentiate successful consultants from their grabby vendor counterparts.

For example, a few years back, I was conducting a selling workshop for a client, and I had what I thought was a stowaway. This guy was not anyone's traditional description of a successful salesperson—soft handshake, not a ton of eye contact, and didn't say a peep in the workshop or contribute much to the small-group discussions. He did, however, approach me at the break and ask for clarification on a couple of points. *Perhaps he's new*, I thought.

When I asked the VP of sales if perhaps this guy was a service tech or a rookie, he laughed out loud (he LOLed, kids). "Jerry is our best salesperson by a huge margin," he snorted. "He's been our top performer in each of the last five years."

That opened my eyes—I spent the rest of the workshop surreptitiously observing this quiet sales Superman. On closer review, he turned out to be an *ambivert*—someone who combines elements of both the introvert and the extrovert and is able to flex and balance their behaviors based on the needs of the situation.

So don't get hung up on whether you're aggressive or outgoing enough—there is room for every kind of style in selling. I'd be more worried about the opposite—are you so much of a driver and go-getter that you're freaking people out?

## Suck Less at Selling:

- If you're an extrovert, be conscious of how your style plays with more introverted customers and temper your exuberant, voluble self accordingly.

- Celebrate and cultivate the qualities of the introvert.

- Seek and value balance and diversity on the sales team—a combination of different styles can result in a sort of collective ambiversion. (It's a word.)

# Know Thyself: Are You Into Relationships or One-Sale Stands?

First, let's be frank: There are two main ways we use the word *love* in modern America—in a *relationship* way and in a *transaction* way.

Relationship *love* implies long-term commitment, growing partnership, and mainly emotional feelings. Transaction *love* implies short-term commitment, temporary partnership, and mainly physical feelings. (In other words, *not* love.)

Was that clinical enough for you? For clarity, here are some examples of the differences in everyday life:

Relationship: "I love you."

Transaction: "I want to make love to you."

Relationship: "Love and Marriage" (Frank Sinatra)

Transaction: "Whole Lotta Love" (Led Zeppelin)

Relationship: "We're in love."

Transaction: "We're lovers."[5]

Whether we're talking about sales or love (and remember, we're talking about both!), there are fundamental and oh-so-important distinctions between these two types of preferences. And your behavior as a seller starts from what you view as your job—are you paid to develop long-term relationships, or are you

---

5. Actually sort of applies to both. This is probably where I should stop.

paid to execute transactions? And how does this line up with your preferences, skills, and motivation? First, let's break it down.

## You're a *relationship* seller if you:

- prefer or excel at long-term commitment
- are good at growing partnerships over time
- derive satisfaction from the emotional feelings of adding value to others
- eventually establish a sole-source relationship with customers
- earn the right to "meet the parents" (executives)
- have the required *emotional qualities* to be effective— empathy, vulnerability, and patience, for starters
- wake up the morning after the sale and start to cook the customer breakfast

## You're a *transactional* seller if you:

- prefer or excel at short-term commitment
- are good at quickly forging temporary partnerships
- derive satisfaction from the physical "rush" of closing
- are not invited to "meet the parents" and don't necessarily care

- have the required *behaviors* to be effective

- wake up the morning after a sale and want to chew your arm off and flee

Both of these selling/loving types aren't necessarily bad; they're just different. The problems start when there's either a fundamental lack of self-awareness and/or a mismatch between your style/preferences and the requirements of the sale. If you don't know what kind of seller you are, you run into problems. And if you're in the wrong job for you, you have real problems.[6]

## Mismatch #1: You're a Transactional Seller in a Relationship Sale

The first mismatch occurs when sellers who prefer the "thrill and kill" of the transaction find themselves in a sale that requires more nurturing and patience. Here are the symptoms:

- You pay way more attention to your next deal than your current deal.

- Your high-base/low-commission pay plan leaves you cold.

- Your customer service sucks.

- Customers leave you just as fast as they join you.

- You never seem to get referrals.

- You can't stand the length of your sales cycle.

---

6.    Wonder how you lean?  Take the quiz at www.loveandselling.com

- Customers are turned off by your premature closing.

- You don't get commissions/bonuses often enough.

For example, my wife, Donna, has a close friend who went from selling advertising space to consulting services . . . and hated it. It's not that she sucked—she was excellent at her job, to the point that she was named Outstanding Newcomer. No doubt she had the skills to succeed.

The problem? She couldn't stand the long sales cycles—she was used to closing something every day, she loved the feeling of counting her money every day, and going weeks without a yes completely freaked her out. As a result, she ended up fighting her natural impulse to close deals, and it created unmanageable stress. So she went back to her old industry, where she's been successfully selling ever since.

Did you ever know someone who was looking for a long-term relationship but mistakenly tried to start one via short-term transactions? Hopefully, you haven't slept with someone on the first date in order to persuade them into a long-term relationship.

## Mismatch #2: You're a Relationship Seller in a Transactional Sale

Here are the symptoms:
- You wish you could see your deals all the way through.

- Your high-commission/low-salary pay plan keeps you awake at night.

- Your customer service is way more awesome than it needs to be.

- Customers love you because you never pressure them . . . and they never buy.

- You never seem to have enough prospects.

- You can't stand the pressure to close.

For example, as interim VP of sales, I once took on a sales-person whose average length of sale was incredibly long. In fact, there was a deal in his funnel that had been "in the works" for eighteen months—for a $100,000 sale! To investigate, we dug into his call outcomes—what were the results of his sales meetings? Almost universally, the answer was "another meeting." The dude couldn't close—his prospects raved about him, but they never seemed to become customers.

Don't look for a steady date in a brothel.

## Find the Sales Job That Fits

If you're a transactional seller, look at sales where buyers are prone to short decision cycles. The more you can hand off service and support to others, the more you can focus on your sweet spot—making sales. To do this, you'll need a steady flow of incoming leads from a well-oiled marketing engine. Add competitive pricing, and you are all set to take advantage of a high commission-to-salary ratio. Just make sure your boss is capable of removing distractions and obstacles.

If you're a relationship seller, you're most likely to be successful in a job with longer sales cycles and more deliberate processes. An established base of customers to nurture will provide both a steady diet of opportunities to up sell/cross sell and the base of referrals and testimonials you use to develop new relationships. A lower commission-to-salary ratio takes the pressure off short-term closing, as does a boss who's good at deflecting executive pressure for numbers in favor of doing the right thing in the long term.

| FIND THE SALES JOB THAT FITS | |
|---|---|
| *Transactional sellers need a job with* | *Relationship sellers need a job with* |
| • short sales cycles | • longer sales cycles |
| • service folks you can hand your customers over to | • an established base of customers to nurture |
| • a steady flow of incoming leads | • a steady flow of opportunities to service and up sell/cross sell |
| • high commission-to-salary ratio | • low commission-to-salary ratio |
| • a boss who understands you and your need to get fed regularly | • a boss who understands you and the nature of the relationship sale |
| • more frequent pipeline reviews | • less frequent pipeline reviews |

## Suck Less at Selling:

- Ask yourself what you really want in a sales job. What part of selling are you passionate about—the thrill of transactional selling or the thrill of relationship selling?

- What's more exciting—hanging out with someone new or doing the Sunday crossword puzzle together?

- Ask yourself what you're really good at. Are you better at prospecting new customers or nurturing existing relationships?

- Are you better at "finding the hook" at the club or picking out that perfect birthday gift?

- Are you in a job that's suited to your inclinations and skills?

- Are you selling in the business equivalent of the night-club or the farmers' market? And how's that working for you?

# The Four Essential Ingredients of Relationship Selling

*Listening*

*Openness*

*Vulnerability*

*Empathy*

Y ou knew the acronym was coming at some point, right? Of course it was! Acronyms help us remember things, they organize complex thoughts, and they're the kind of catchy stuff you expect from a guy who has to hold salespeople's attention for a living.

This is one acronym, though, that I didn't have to force or stretch to make my point. Consider each component:

## Listening

*Listening* is two things. First, it's an attitude great sellers bring to their work every day. Sellers with a desire to understand listen more often and more deeply than their less-effective counterparts.

Donna is quite adept at discerning when I *want* to listen and when I am just listening because that's what spouses are supposed to do. I can think I'm using all the right behaviors, but intent (or lack of it) is either the perfume or the stink that she picks up on.

Second, listening is the behavior that unlocks relationships and enables the other essential behaviors. If I'm not listening, I'm not open. I'm not being vulnerable. I'm not in an empathetic state of mind. We'll go into the difference between cursory listening and truly listening to understand later.

Third, listening shows you care. And it's easier for people to care about people who care about them.

## Openness

*Openness* is also two things. First, it's functioning without concealment or hiding, operating without an ulterior motive. In the excellent book *Getting to Yes*, Fisher and Ury say that the key to successful negotiating lies not in hiding your interests but in sharing them openly and encouraging the other party to do the same. I believe the same is true throughout the selling process—being open about your interests and needs lowers the barrier to allow trust and encourages reciprocal behavior from customers.

Donna absolutely knows when I'm asking leading questions in a shallow attempt to manipulate her toward the outcome I secretly want. Here's an example:

**Me:** "Man, the Packers are doing great this season."

**Donna:** "Mmm."

**Me:** "How long has it been since I've been to a game?"

**Donna:** "Okay, when's the game?"

(**Author's note:** I rarely do this.)

(**Donna's note:** Dan always does this.)

Secondly, openness is a willingness or readiness to receive. I don't just mean receive the order. I mean receiving criticism, objections, and learning points without defensiveness. Openness and listening are interdependent—if you're not open, you're not really listening. Some of the most challenging moments in selling are when customers criticize or object to your offering—are you open to the learning, or are you preparing your rebuttal?

Of course, the most striking opportunity to exhibit openness is when facing customer objections. Sellers who are open to customer feedback cherish objections as information to ingest, not points to be argued.

## Vulnerability

*Vulnerability* is a state of being susceptible to attack, to being wounded or hurt. And why, you ask, would a seller want that?

Of course I don't want you to get hurt. The point is really about trust—putting yourself in that position with another person sends a powerful message that you trust them. And if you want someone, particularly a customer, to be vulnerable to you, you need to lead the dance.

For sellers, that means things like admitting you don't know, like letting customers see the faults and challenges with your offering, like letting them into the "back room" so they can really understand how your company works and how you make money. When a customer knows your margins, are you susceptible to price negotiations? Yes, you are, and you need to be extremely judicious about disclosing things like that.[7] But if you want to know their real budget, there may be value in taking that risk, in making yourself vulnerable.

## Empathy

*Empathy* is understanding and being sensitive to the feelings of another person. Do you understand the needs and feelings of another person? Do you recognize the situation they believe they're in? Are you hearing their story or telling your own? Empathy isn't good listening; it's *why* you listen to customers—because you want to truly get it.

Example: If I hear every word someone says to me to the point I can repeat it back, but I miss the emotions behind the words, have I really listened? The late, great Stephen Covey notes that the result of true listening is when you can play back what the other person *means*, not just what they *said*.

Of course, there's more to love than LOVE, but these four ingredients are absolutely essential in both love and selling. Trying to grow and sustain a healthy relationship without them is like trying to bake a cake without butter—what comes out may be edible, but it sure ain't cake.

## Suck Less at Selling:

- To complete the listening process, reflect back what the customer means.

---

7.  Sales managers: I did *not* just instruct your salespeople to divulge your pricing strategy. Although some very successful companies do exactly that.

- First, master your own stories, assumptions, and prejudices. Then you're ready.

- Be open about your agenda and your intentions, and ask for the same from customers.

- Be vulnerable if you want others to be vulnerable. You go first.

- Once you smell what the customer is stepping in, you're ready to start helping.

# The World's Most Underrated Sales Expert

One of the most *underrated* books of all time for sales professionals is *The Five Love Languages* by Gary Chapman. If you've read it, consider the application to sales as you run through this section. If you haven't read it, I highly recommend it.

The headlines: Everyone has a preferred way to give/receive love—a primary "love language." Our preferred "language" is a combination of natural preference and how we were taught. When we communicate love in the other person's language, they feel it. When we communicate it in a language other than their natural one, they don't feel it. It's like we're speaking to them in a foreign language.

Therefore, if developing relationships is important to you, you must understand both your own and the other person's love languages. It's essential that you become proficient at "speaking" each of the five love languages.

Now substitute the word *selling* for the word *love* in the above paragraphs, and you have one of the world's most underrated sales books.

**Why It Could Matter to You:** When you understand and focus on "showing the love" the way customers want it, you can sell to a wider variety of people. Inflexible or under-skilled salespeople often have limited success, because they can't find enough prospects with whom they naturally align. Take any highly successful salesperson, and I'll wager you are looking at someone who has unlocked the code of dealing with people who differ. (Or they were in the right place at the right time—luck happens.)

Let's take a brief tour through Chapman's love languages and discuss sales applications.[8]

## Love Language: Words of Affirmation

Gary Chapman's first love language is words of affirmation. Those are straightforward verbal expressions in support of the other person. They deposit currency in the other person's emotional bank account.

Most of you are confident in your ability to use language to make a connection and help a customer feel good about buying from you. After all, your fantastic interviewing skills are what got you hired in the first place, yes?

## Classic Sales Error #1: Excessive Self-Affirmation

I've found many sellers use more words to affirm *themselves* than they do to affirm the *customer*. They make statements like these:

- "You are really going to improve X with my solution."

- "Our customers achieve consistently measurable results."

- "This is a fantastic value/deal/offer."

8. Everything in this section depends on good intent, the desire to help customers. If you're just trying to manipulate your way to a sale, please put this book down. It's not for you.

- "The benefits of my solution are . . ."
- "What that means to you is . . ."

So what's wrong with these? Isn't this what salespeople are paid to do? Well, let's break these down by looking at them through the **Lens of Love**, and you tell me.

- "You are going to love me."
- "My previous dates/spouses are measurably better for having known me."
- "I am fantastic."
- "The benefits of dating me are . . ."
- "What dating me means to you is . . ."

The problem: All of these are seller- and solution-centric. You're pointing your affirming language back at yourself. And that's cheesy-seller territory.

## Classic Sales Error #2: Schmoozing (a.k.a. the Eddie Haskell)[9]

Young folks, go to Wikipedia and look up "Eddie Haskell" a very definition of *sycophant*. (In other words, "transparent kiss-ass.") Unfortunately, many of you have been trained to do the Eddie Haskell under the guise of building rapport.

---

9. Would somebody please write *The Sales Wisdom of Beaver Cleaver*, or do I have to do it?

Eddie Haskell: "What a lovely suit you're wearing today, Mrs. Cleaver."

Seller (noticing mounted fish on the prospect's wall): "Nice fish. Where'd you catch it?"

These two statements differ not at all in their intent—you're searching out something to compliment in the hopes of building rapport so you can get something you want. Unfortunately, if your customer is not into that love language or is not easily fooled, you are appearing to butter them up or schmooze them. Not good.

Chapman advises you to do more than pay compliments to your customers. He recommends three additional levels of affirming words:

1. **Encouraging words.** These are statements that affirm the other person's ability to do, be, and accomplish things to which they aspire. This is a good thing to do if you rely on internal selling and motivated buyers.

2. **Kind words.** Even difficult conversations can be viewed as affirming when the tone is one of kindness and respect. This is particularly important when negotiations get tough.

3. **Humble words.** This is making humble requests versus demands. This is your ability to take responsibility and not shift blame. It employs the power of a sincere apology and the desire to make amends. These are valuable words in selling, particularly if you're trying to build a lasting customer relationship.

## Building Rapport or Schmoozing?

Understanding your customer's preferences is key to using the right mix of love languages. Here's a handy guide to determine whether you are connecting or wasting your time.

**If someone values words of affirmation, they will use words themselves**—they pay a lot of compliments. These folks will give you more feedback on where you stand and what they like about your offering. And if this is your love language too, they will make you feel good—sometimes to the point of lulling you into a false sense of security.

**If someone does *not* value words of affirmation, they will be suspicious of and put off by any hint of the Eddie Haskell.** They seldom give you enough feedback on where you stand and will provide less feedback on the relative strengths of your proposal. As a result, they maintain maximum negotiating leverage. Finally, if words of affirmation are your language, these folks are difficult to sell to—it seems cold or distant.

## The Infatuation Trap

Using words of affirmation is easy when the relationship is new—we pay each other more compliments when we're first dating, and we compliment the new customer more on their effectiveness. It's also more likely to happen when we're pursuing an objective. For example, my spouse observes that I say nicer things to her when I want something. . . and she may have a point.

The key is consistency. Do you use the right love languages over time? How about when things are not rosy? Or when you're not trying to sell something? Consistency is vital to relationship sustainability.

## Love Language: Quality Time

By quality time, Chapman means three things: (1) Spending time focusing on each other, (2) having quality conversations, and (3) doing things together. Pardon me for noticing, but that looks a lot like what a lot of consultative sellers are (and mostly should be) seeking to do.

So let's look at each aspect of quality time and see 1) the right way and 2) how each aspect is most often translated incorrectly by sellers:

**Focusing on each other.** Even when engaged in an activity (e.g., golf), the focus needs to be on each other. That gives you the best chance of sharing quality time. Key words: *each other*. Just like in love, each person has needs that must ultimately be met and viewpoints that are valuable to share.

**Classic Sales Error:** Whether you're in a business meeting, at dinner, or on the golf course, the temptation is to focus on the business . . . or more specifically, the sales opportunity. That's particularly true when it seems like the only thing you have in common is the business. But if you're more focused on the golf than the customer, you're missing the point of quality time.

Excessive focus on the business and not enough on the customer is like paying more attention to the dinner than your date.

**Quality conversations.** Gary Chapman says, "A relationship calls for sympathetic listening with a view to understanding the other person's thoughts, feelings, and desires. We must be willing to give advice but only when it is requested and never in a condescending manner." Mr. Chapman might as well be your sales manager talking.

**Classic Sales Error:** Again, I go to Gary Chapman: "We are trained to analyze problems and create solutions. We forget that [it's] a relationship, not a project to be completed or a problem to solve."

The reason many would-be consultative sellers fail at consultative selling is *narrow focus*. You're so laser-focused on your sales opportunity and the close that you lose sight of the customer's personal needs. I've witnessed plenty of sellers whose implication/consequence questions focused everywhere *except* how the customer was personally affected by things.

Focusing too much on your sales opportunity at the expense of the customer is like spending your dinner date talking about the getting down you're hoping to do later.

**Quality activities.** Here we're talking about doing things together that are enjoyable because you're doing them together. Those activities are all the more meaningful when they're enjoyable to your customer. The trick in business, of course, is to make every moment count for the business—we're talking about relevant activities like attending a workshop together. Fewer customers than ever have time to take in a ball game.

**Classic Sales Error:** Many sales organizations make the fatal mistake of neglecting the activities that helped to win the business. In love, this would be like getting married and then refusing to go on dates with your spouse. Think about it: once the contract is won, does the customer see your executives as often? How often are the engineers "getting together" these days? When was the last time you had a nonbusiness conversation with the customer?

In love, when you strip away the dating, you are left with operating reality and problems to solve—boring at best, contentious and dysfunctional at worst. You know what makes a lot of that stuff go away or matter less—if you're still doing the stuff that made you love each other to begin with.

Stopping the activities that won you the business is like letting yourself go right after the honeymoon and gaining fifty pounds. 'Nuff said.

## Effective Use of the Triple L (Lunch, Links, and Liquor)[10]

So how does this apply to the sacred perks of selling, the T&E budget, and ultimately the cost of sales? Of course I have thoughts on this:

Be sensitive to the cultural norms and individual preferences of your customers. Not everyone wants to go to a strip club.

Look for events that customers truly enjoy, not just the events your company has tickets to. Yes, you love golf . . . but does your customer?

Emphasize active over passive events—it's better to do something than watch something.

---

10. For those of you with no travel-and-expense budget, salespeople in past times often took their customers golfing, eating, and drinking. This still happens on Wall Street and at executive levels.

Emphasize meals—breaking bread is a powerful connector of people. Plus, people gotta eat.

I'm not even gonna touch the subject of liquor, and I rarely touch the liquor itself. Suffice to say I know of several business relationships (and marriages) that were founded upon drinking . . . and dissolved the same way. Proceed with caution.

Above all, pay attention to your customers. Do they value quality time? Are they into quality conversation? What do they truly like to do? What would make your time together more than just the typical buyer/seller dance?

## Love Language: Gifts

Here, we'll look at one of the most time-honored customs in selling.[11] I'm talking about bribing your custo—er, I mean, giving gifts. (To be clear: Bribery is wrong. Don't do it.)

Gifts are vital symbols of many companies' sales strategies. You see them everywhere, from the trinkets that lure you into the trade show booth to the gift baskets that pile up at the holidays. In between, there's the SWAG (Stuff We All Get) and the more precious gifts reserved for the special few clients.

I have a customer's perspective on this: My dad, Carl, managed transportation and logistics for a manufacturing company in Milwaukee when I was growing up. As such, he bought a lot of rail and trucking services. And transportation is an industry where gift giving is a mandatory cost of doing business. As a result, Dad got a lot of stuff. A whole lot.

11. This is changing somewhat—many companies now have policies against employees receiving gifts from vendors.

But does it work? Or is it seen as bribery? Does it help vendors win the business, or is it money wasted?[12]

The key, as we've discussed, is whether gifts are the primary love language of the customer. Does the customer really appreciate and value gifts, or are they merely eating your candy? If they value gifts, then yours will be received with heartfelt gratitude, and relationships will be strengthened. If not, you are simply adding to the cost of sales and reducing profits. It's important to read the person—not all customers value gifts equally, and not all customers will require or deserve the same level of gifting.

## Three Keys for Making Gifts Matter

**Key #1: Make It Matter to the Customer.** My dad got a ton of gifts—everything from hats to fireworks (really). However, the gifts that mattered most to him were tickets to sporting events. Why? It allowed him to take *me*—he was able to give me a gift, which he valued most. Some of our best memories as father and son were courtesy of vendors, and those vendors did a lot of business with my dad. Correlation or causality? You be the judge. All I know for sure is I saw some great games.

**Key #2: Make It Unique.** I vividly recall the giant pile of logoed hats and pens in our house. Even for a kid, they quickly lost value. The more hats and pens, the less any individual hat and pen stood out. If you are giving a gift that everyone else is giving, you are not building value or gaining competitive

---

12. Of course, I am sensitive to cultural norms and the gift *requirement* in many countries and sales. Don't stop gifting if it's a cultural norm—we're talking about the discretionary gifting that sellers use to gain an advantage.

advantage. At best, you are staying even. The solution is to find something unique—that no one else is giving and that is also valued by the customer.

**Key #3: Make an Effort.** The level of personal effort goes a long way toward making your gift matter. Think about it. If you're a parent, what is more meaningful: A) a gift your child buys for you, or B) a gift the child makes for you? If you said B, you get it. If you said A, perhaps gifts are not your primary love language, eh?

Again, it all starts with understanding your customer. What is their primary language? What is personally meaningful to them?

## Love Language: Acts of Service

This love language, which is essentially *doing things* for the customer to show them love, is the most underrated and under-leveraged love language for many sellers. It's misinterpreted as "customer service." It's viewed as "going the extra mile." It commonly takes the form of heroic efforts that move heaven and earth and sometimes stretch company rules. Plus, many of you have "people" for the customer service part. You're a hunter, not a farmer, damn it!

**Classic Sales Error:** It's easy to focus on the big, dramatic things and miss the little, day-to-day things, particularly if this is not your primary love language. Yes, you got your company to make a major exception, put a rush on something, or something similar. You spent a lot of money to fly out there at a crucial point in the deal cycle. You came through in a crisis. But are you doing the things that show personal care and concern on a daily basis? Are you spending your own time and not just company time and money? Many customers' most lasting relationships with sellers are founded on the "little things." Like getting back to customers in a timely manner.

Focusing on the "big splash" acts of service at the expense of the everyday is like making your spouse a nine-course dinner on your anniversary . . . then leaving the toilet seat up. (Again, fellas, I'm mostly talking to you here. Ladies, you could perhaps consider leaving the seat up on occasion.)

## Love Language: Physical Touch

I'm not even gonna . . . touch this one. Your HR department will have a better . . . feel for this topic. Instead of a book, you might find a resource with a more . . . hands-on approach.[13]

## Suck Less at Selling:

- Read *The Five Love Languages* by Gary Chapman. Then read it again.

- Understand your own dialect—what do you prefer?

- Consider your blind spots. Where do you overapply a language? What languages do you underutilize because they are not natural?

---

13. Thank you! I'm here all week! Tip your servers!

- Seek to understand the language of your customer—how do they prefer their love?

- Focus on giving customers what they need to feel the love, even if it's not natural for you. After all, you're the one who's paid to adapt, not them.

# Who Do Buyers Trust?

*Trust is the fruit of a relationship
in which you know you are loved.*

—WILLIAM PAUL YOUNG

Trust is a beautiful thing in professional selling—it's the key that unlocks long-term, mutually beneficial relationships in both business and life. Let's start by defining this beautiful thing.

- When customers trust you, they have confidence in what you say and in your ability to make good on your word.

- When customers trust you, they rely on your ability to help them—through your solutions, your sales process, or both.

And when this trust happens, doing business gets a lot easier. Customers operate on good faith, because they're confident you're doing the same. Customers can take your word to the bank, and handshakes suffice where contracts would normally be required.[14] Advocates sell on your behalf within their organizations. Faults, shortcomings, and temporary failings are forgiven. Anxious inspection and verification give way to calm assurance that things are happening as they should.

---

14. Note that I am in favor of a good, solid contract where possible.

In fact, this sounds a lot like a great loving relationship, doesn't it? (Is it too early in this section to look through the Lens of Love? No, it is not!) A relationship built on trust is durable in so many ways that I get emotional just thinking about it.

The problem: You don't start there, and it's exceedingly difficult and somewhat rare to get there. It's as high as a mountain and, ah, more difficult to ascend. And sales as a profession has a lot to do with that—for generations, sellers been viewed as sleazy, cheesy, and easy. You'll say anything and do anything to get the sale. Your own commission matters more than customer needs. You overpromise and under-deliver. Well, not you, but people you know and people that have come before you. Sales has evolved, but in this case, dinosaurs still roam the earth, giving selling a bad name.

To illustrate this point, let's use a model—the LOVE LADDER. Each of us has a mental ladder that we use to compare data sources. Which ones do we trust more or less? In my experience, there is never a tie; just like on a real ladder, no two people can occupy the same rung. Somebody always outranks or is outranked by another. For instance, you love/trust one news source or political candidate more or less than another. There are no ties.

Example: The prospect is planning on taking the safe, known course of renewing their current vendor arrangement for another year. You are the competing vendor hoping they change their mind and take the risk of investing with you. It will be worth it, of course!

Think about all the ways the customer could hear the opinion, "Take a risk and go with the new vendor." Think of all the sources: you (the new vendor), your technical expert (example: application engineer), your boss (VP sales), other customers of yours (testimonials/case studies), the prospect's peers within the company, industry experts (third parties), empirical data (research or test data), and the prospect's own beliefs (their "gut," or the "little voice in their head").

Now, I've observed countless—literally, I stopped counting after a while—sales processes spanning numerous industries, verticals, types, lengths, and levels. Here's the sequence in which these different data points are typically involved/employed by the seller:

1.  Sellers offer benefit statements based on their needs assessment

2.  Sellers bring in the technical expert for support

3.  Sellers share case studies and testimonials

4.  Sellers bring in their boss

5.  Sellers point to research and data . . . conducted or compiled by the seller

6.  Sellers leverage internal advocates

7.  Sellers get a reaction from the customer

I've also asked countless sellers and customers how they would rank each of the above data points on the customer's LOVE LADDER. Think about it. If you were a customer wondering whether to change vendors, and each of these data points was saying, "Change," while the others were saying, "Don't change," which sources do you love and trust more? (Because this is a thought experiment, imagine each of these data points is equally known to you—you haven't had a twenty-year relationship with any one of them.)

Here's how both customers *and* sellers tend to rank the customer's LOVE LADDER:

- Their own beliefs

- Peers within the company

- Other customers

- Industry experts

- Data

- Seller's technical expert

- Salesperson

- VP of sales

Don't believe me? Of course not! I'm the seller here, trying to sell my point! Look at where I am on your LOVE LADDER!

To help you get your mind around this concept, let's look again through the Lens of Love. (For purposes of discussion, we will use the boys-pursuing-girls metaphor. Saves a lot of unwieldy his/her, s/he crap.)

You, the fella, are out with your fellas. You are chatting up a lady you like. She is currently casually seeing someone. You would like her to ditch her current date and leave the club with you. How would her LOVE LADDER look on this topic? I'll take a guess:

- Her own opinion/belief
- Her friends' opinions
- Your ex-girlfriend vouching for you
- Someone who knows both of you
- Your Facebook page/eHarmony profile
- Your married friends
- You

Whether we're talking about business or love, the point is clear—whoever is trying to "make the sale" is, by definition, suspect and thus ranks relatively low on the Ladder.

But *why* is it this way?

There are two fundamental reasons our ladders stack the way they do, both in business and in love. I'll define them, and then we'll resume the analogy stretching.

## Principle #1: Confirmation Bias—We Love Our Own Data the Most

**Definition:** Confirmation bias describes our tendency to seek data that confirms our beliefs and to avoid data that contradicts our beliefs. It's like a filter that lets agreeable information in but keeps disagreeable information out. You've probably heard it described as "looking at the world through rose-colored glasses"—everything looks rosy when viewed through that filter. If you describe someone's glass as half-empty or half-full, you're describing their confirmation bias—toward the negative or the positive.

**Business Example:** While traveling with a medical device sales rep, I once heard a cardiologist say, "I love data . . . as long as it's consistent with my own data." Have you ever experienced a customer who went their own way despite a chorus of protests from all around them? People simply don't argue with their own data as much as they should.

When you're in the infatuation stage of love (you know, the mushy, romantic kind), who is going to tell you that you're making a mistake? Nobody! You're not listening! True story: When Donna and I got married, we asked our pastor, Dave, if he was going to give us some premarital counseling. He declined, saying, "You're in love. You're not listening. Come back in a year, and we'll see." Danged if he wasn't right about that.

**Summary:** Confirmation bias is why sellers who offer unwanted, contradictory advice often find themselves shut out, objected to, and kicked out. It's also why the infatuation stage of love is so dang awesome—you're in love! Everything is beautiful, even if it's not.

## Principle #2: Narrative Fallacy—We Love Our Stories More Than Reality

**Definition:** Narrative fallacy describes our tendency to adopt stories, or narratives, that explain events in a way that conforms to our confirmation bias. Humans have an innate need to explain things in a narrative form; it's how we mentally make sense of a chaotic, seemingly random world. Oftentimes, this leads to people lying to themselves in search of an answer—hence the *fallacy* part. Customers will refute your empirical data (example: pilot test results) because it contradicts their views. Because they don't trust you, the seller, they will explain away the data.

**Business Example:** I have conducted hundreds, if not thousands, of postmortem "loss evaluations" with salespeople who just failed to win a deal. In 98 percent of the cases, salespeople ascribe their loss to either the customer's shortcomings ("They just don't get the value") or the failure of their solution ("Our price was too high"). Rarely, if ever, have I heard a version of "I didn't do a good enough job of understanding their needs" or "I offered solutions prematurely." Ooh, but why did we win the deal? Superior selling, of course!

The psychologist John Gottman uses the terms *positive sentiment override* and *negative sentiment override* to describe the way our confirmation bias creates the narrative fallacy. For example, if you're in infatuation-driven positive sentiment override, your glass is half-full. You're looking at me through rose-colored glasses, and everything is rosy. There's nothing I can do that you can't explain away. Did I stand you up for a date? I must be busy and overworked. Did I insult you? I'm just tired.

On the other hand, if you're in negative sentiment override, your glass is half-empty as it relates to me. Even my best actions will look fishy to you. Did I bring you flowers? I must be angling for something. Did I say something nice to you? I must have meant it sarcastically. In negative sentiment override, there's nothing I can do that can't be painted with the evil brush.

**Summary:** Even data and experience will not sway customers who have a set-in-stone view of the world, especially if it's coming from you, the seller. That leads us to our third principle . . .

## Principle #3: Law of Like Agendas—We Love People Like Us

**Definition:** Customers trust people who share their agenda and tend to trust those with competing agendas somewhat less. Did you notice the groupings in the LOVE LADDER? For most customers, there's a definite line of demarcation that can be explained by this law.

**Bonus—Animal Kingdom Example:** Zebras would put other zebras toward the top of their Zebra Ladder. Why? They share the same agenda: avoiding being eaten. On the other hand, hyenas would rank much lower on the Zebra Ladder—the hyena agenda is all about eating zebras. And that's the way most customers view you (at least at first): as a hyena trying to eat their wallet. So the zebras herd together and take pains to avoid the hyenas. That's why customers tend to roam in small herds at trade shows, grazing at your bowl of free candy, keeping a wary eye on you, and running at the first sound of "Hey, how you doin'?"

This is why all the single ladies go to the club in small herds. They even go to the bathroom in pairs! (Can I tack on a Lens of Love to an animal kingdom example? Yes, I can!)

So, how do you apply the principles of confirmation bias, like agendas, and narrative fallacy?

**References Beat Testimonials:** The law of like agendas explains why it's so important to have a significant portfolio of references—customers who are willing to talk with your prospects. References totally beat testimonials, which are letters from satisfied customers. Why? Because your testimonial is carefully selected data furnished by you, the seller (and probably edited to make you shine, says the wary zebra customer). References, on the other hand, involve direct conversation with another customer.

The boy or girl you are pursuing would *love* to talk with your last boyfriend/girlfriend. You would not hand them an undated testimonial letter.

**Develop an Internal Advocate:** You know what would let you into the herd? If one of the zebras told their buddies that you weren't such a bad hyena after all. And that you were a vegan.

At the club, it helps if one of her friends is telling her to go for it.[15]

---

15. Again, this works in all sorts of ways—I'm just using the "boy pursues girl" version because it's easier and more obvious.

**Bring (or Send) a Technical Expert:** When faced with the choice of believing you or your engineer, most customers choose the engineer. They're perceived as more truthful than the seller. Why? Because their agenda more closely resembles the customer's—they want the solution to work too (whereas you may just be after their wallet).

Example: I once spent months and months (and many dollars) wooing a big, juicy medical device prospect when I sold in the technical research sector. I took them to dinner, got to know them personally, got our families together . . . only to be cast aside the moment they met my application engineer. I got demoted to third-wheel status the moment they found someone with a more alike agenda.

My best wingman ever was a wing*woman*. Best zebra ever.

$$Trust = \frac{1}{Quota}$$

**Leave Your Sales Boss at the Office:** A lot of you bring your boss to key customer meetings to "show customers the love" or "demonstrate the company's commitment." But is that how customers view it? Unfortunately, no—to the zebra, your sales boss just looks like a faster, hungrier hyena. That's because trust is inversely related to quota—the more quota you carry, the more likely your agenda is to close. (That's also why the quotaless technical expert outranks you on the Ladder.) Your bosses have a bigger quota than you. They're not paid to stay around and take care of the customer. In fact, the minute they're done here, they're moving on to the next ~~kill~~ closing opportunity.

care of the customer. In fact, the minute they're done here, they're moving on to the next ~~kill~~ closing opportunity.

Plus, the later you involve your sales bosses, the more likely they are to be viewed with suspicion. Closing time? Here comes the big hyena. End of the quarter? Bring on the superhyenas!

Bringing in your sales boss to help you close the deal is like having your mom show up at the club just as the lights are going up. I'm just saying that move may entail a certain amount of risk.[16]

## Painful Illustrations of the LOVE LADDER in Action

To illustrate how amazingly powerful the LOVE LADDER is, let's play a little game. I'll ask you some questions, and you raise or lower your hand depending on your answer. If you're in public, you may want to do this mentally.

1.  Raise your hand if you've ever had the "Don't do it!" talk with a friend or loved one who was about to make an extremely poor relationship decision (example: marry that loser).

    *   In my workshops, several hands usually go up—I'm amazed at how many of us have attempted this very dangerous conversation.

---

16. If you put your ear right up to this book and listen really hard, you can hear the analogy screaming a tiny scream as it's stretched to the breaking point.

2. Keep your hand up if the person in question changed their mind and called off the wedding because of your advice.

   - Most of you just put your hand down.

3. Put your hand back up if they *should have* taken your advice—results proved you correct.

   - Most of you just emphatically thrust your arm skyward. A significant percentage of you raised both hands.

4. Keep your hand up if you weren't the only one telling them not to do it.

   - Almost all your hands are still up.

5. Keep your hand up if the person in question ignored facts and evidence that proved you right.

   - Your arms are getting tired from holding them up. You may rest.

I hear some amazing stories from workshop participants—with some very salacious (and extremely fun) details. I'll summarize them here into a composite example that should resemble yours:

Your close friend Sam is infatuated with the Wrong Person and ready to propose marriage. Sam's friends are all saying, "Don't do it!" but their advice is ignored (confirmation bias). Sam's parents are threatening to disown, but it doesn't matter. A warning from the Wrong Person's ex (law of like agendas) also makes no difference. Photographs of the Wrong Person making out with someone else "have obviously been photoshopped" (narrative fallacy). In other words, there's nothing that will dissuade Sam from making the wrong choice—Sam's data rules, and bad decisions often ensue.

This Lens of Love example is remarkably like the sob story I've heard from a lot of sellers. A new executive comes in, and you're out as a vendor, despite years of successful implementations. Your internal advocates are appalled, but there's nothing they can do. Your testimonials and your boss have no effect. Your track record of results is ignored in favor of a "fresh approach." Everyone hates the decision, but the new executive is intent on making his mark.

The point: The LOVE LADDER and the principles it contains are powerful stuff. Sometimes there is nothing you can do except recognize it . . . and wait.

## How Sellers Make It Worse

Sellers add to the problem in a variety of ways. I'll just hit the highlights here and offer antidotes, perhaps with a little Lens of Love/animal kingdom thrown in to keep your attention.

## Problem #1: Sellers Lead with Their Own Agendas

Even your meeting agenda says a lot about who you're focused on. Hint: If your meeting agenda contains nouns about your solution or their buying process, that's a tip-off. They're usually about your agenda. Other hint: If your first questions are about qualifying the customer (in other words, your need to sell), that smells like hyenas talking. The most classic example of this is the trial close—"If I could show you something that would meet all your needs, would you buy from me?" Ah, no. No, I wouldn't.

**Solution: Lead with the customer's agenda.** Your meeting agenda should be about their needs and what they're trying to *do* (verb). Lead with questions about their needs. Start by talking zebra talk.

You tell me what's a better first-date strategy: qualifying them, trial closing them, or asking about what they like to do?

## Problem #2: Sellers Make "Benefit Statements"

You know, traditional sales—school stuff like "The benefit of our solution is . . ." and "What this means to you is . . ." and "You'll save time/money/hassle, be more effective, and so on . . ." The problem is not the content of your statements; it's who's making them. You're the last one who should be saying that stuff. It's like the hyena trying to convince the zebras. Do the zebras trust the hyena's benefit statements?

**Antidote: Customers determine their own benefits.** Ask the questions that get them to figure it out. Challenge customers to define what the outcomes or value might be. If they say it, they own it and believe it.

Would you say things like "Here's what dating me will do for you," or would you want your prospective honey to determine that? Think hard about that one.

## Problem #3: Making Value Judgments for the Customer

When you say things like "This is a fair deal" or "Our solution is an excellent value," you're presenting a value judgment. Hopefully by this point in the book, you're thinking that may not be so wise. In fact, customers will often actively look for reasons you're wrong.

**Antidote: Let the customers make their own judgments.** Ask them for a reaction. Find out what they think. Withhold your own judgment in favor of hearing theirs—after all, their judgment rules.

You don't have a "funny story"—you have a story. I'll decide if it's funny. Going out with you may or may not be a "great time"—I'll decide, thank you very much.

## Problem #4: Relying on Testimonials

Yes, testimonials are ostensibly customer data, but they're provided by you, the seller. The skeptical customer might say, "Of course you have selected the one customer who didn't have a sucky experience." Or, "I see there's no date on this. When's this from, 1985?" Or even, "I see you edited all the bad stuff out." In fact, early in my career, I worked for a company who did all that.

**Antidote: Provide references, good and bad.** If you're really confident in your solution, you should welcome the opportunity to connect future customers with current customers. If you're up front and honest (thus more trustworthy), you are okay with letting customers see both sides of you, the great and not so great. In fact, offering a balanced view increases the likelihood that you look less like a hyena. More than ever, customers are requiring (and checking) a balanced set of references.

Your prospective honey is messaging your former lovers to get the straight poop on you. That's the way the world works now.

## The Key to Leveraging the Ladder: Questions

Questions reveal the customer's confirmation bias. Questions involve high-trust data sources. Questions get customers to create their own narratives. Questions help you align with the law of like agendas. And questions keep your statements and value judgments to a minimum.

## Q and A: Sellers Attempt to Refute the LOVE LADDER

**Q:** But Dan, my customers have known me for years. They invite me to their barbecues. They name their pets after me. They trust me, and they know they can take my advice to the bank.

**A:** Congratulations! That's hard to achieve, and usually the result of a lot of time, effort, and right behaviors. Two points: But, the LOVE LADDER is relative, not absolute. Just because you rank low doesn't mean you're not trustworthy. In this example, what you've done is lower the barrier of mistrust— you haven't necessarily outranked anyone. And that barrier can be raised again in a heartbeat.

**Q:** But Dan, customers love it when I bring my bosses. They like "getting the love" from my VIPs.

**A:** Of course they do—your bosses have more power, can make more exceptions, and typically come with a fancier dinner and a more expensive bottle of wine. That doesn't necessarily mean customers *trust* them more.

**Q:** But Dan, some of my customers love me more than they trust their own coworkers. How about that, smarty-pants?

**A:** That's typically the law of like agendas coming into play— the customer distrusts their peers' agendas for political or competitive reasons. Good selling by you too!

**Q:** But Dan, I once talked a loved one out of marrying the Wrong Person.

**A:** I've occasionally heard these examples. In most cases, the loved one already has a question in their mind that opens them to your confirming advice. Someone who asks you, "Am I making the right choice here?" is already questioning their own bias. And in a lot of cases, there's other data there. I'm sure you're überpersuasive, but it's usually not just you.

**Suck Less at Selling:**
- Get the customer to say it if you want them to own it.
- Speak through colleagues, peers, and other zebras.
- When at all possible, keep your hyena mouth shut.
- Take all the words you use to attach your value to things . . . and put them away.

# PART
# TWO

*Looking for Love, a.k.a. Prospecting*

# There Are No Blind Dates

When I first had the idea for this book, I was totally looking forward to writing about blind dates—the tragedy, the triumph, and of course the incredible awkwardness.

Unfortunately, since that time, the blind date has become extinct. Its killer: the Internet. Just as humans have killed off the mighty (but too trusting) dodo bird, the Internet has killed off the idea of blindly trusting your friend's/coworker's/meddling aunt's assurances that "you two will hit it off."

The same holds true in business. The sales version of the blind date—the customer is willing to meet with you to learn about you—is gone forever. Nowadays, thanks again to the Internet, you and your solutions are researched, vetted, and qualified—or disqualified—before anyone lets you in the door.

Let's break down the differences between then (Dark Ages) and now (Internet Age), again employing that most useful of sales devices, the Lens of Love.

How it used to work: Customers were willing to meet with you because they needed to learn more about the product or service you're selling. You were the vehicle by which they learned what they needed to know to qualify or disqualify you. At best, the customer had heard about you through a colleague that had experience with you and could provide a solid referral. Often, that was not the case—the customer was going in blind.

Your prospective mate had to actually go out with you to learn more about you. The blind date was how they learned whether you were cool or a freak. At best, the friend/coworker/meddling aunt that connected you actually knew something about the two of you. Often, that was not the case—Aunt Nellie simply thought the two of you would look good together, and after all, you're not getting any younger.

Needless to say, the results were mixed. In my sales training workshops, I've often asked participants to recount their best/ worst blind-date experiences. Of course, the kids don't exactly know what I'm talking about, but the more "seasoned" folks have some amazing stories to tell—both heartwarming and tragic. For every "love at first sight" story, there are at least two "I couldn't wait to get out of there" stories.

In sales, the story was the same—for every first prospect meeting that went well, there were typically a couple where the seller walked out thinking, *There's an hour of my life I can never get back.* It was an uncomfortable feeling indeed to realize in the middle of the meeting that there's somewhere better you could be. I know. When my sales career began, the Internet was a fledgling—we hadn't even heard of MySpace yet. (Cue the kids asking, "What's MySpace?")

How it works now: The customer has people (sometimes consultants—we'll get to that later) that conduct an initial scan of the marketplace as part of their procurement management process. They research your products and services via your website. They compare you to your competitors using online research tools like Hoover's or Dun & Bradstreet. They look at customer review websites to see what your customers have said about you. They look at your company's profile to learn who's who. They look at your LinkedIn profile to see what you're all about. They may even use your website's helpful tools to receive initial product/service information—sometimes all the way up to a price quote. Then, if you've passed through all those gates (company, product/solution, customers, you), you get to meet.

Your prospective mate goes to the online dating sites to see where you've put it out there. They check out your Facebook profile and Twitter feed to see if you're a freak or a potential match. They look at your timeline to see who you've dated before and whether they recognize anybody. They Google you to see who's flamed you. They run a criminal background check to find out if you're a felon (although that may not disqualify you). They look at your Facebook friends and visit their pages to see if you come from a family of freaks or if you hang out with freaks. They check who you're following on Twitter to see if you have good taste. If you pass all those tests, you get a date.[17]

In other words, things have completely flipped from then to now. Here's what else has changed about prospecting in the Internet Age.

**Referrals have been supplemented by reviews**. In the old days, customers often relied on the advice/recommendation of a single colleague when making the decision to meet you. Now, thanks to the Internet, they can learn the opinion of every customer who cares enough to post a review online, tag you on Facebook, or hashtag you on Twitter.

---

17. There is also this thing called "Privacy Settings" that you should get familiar with.

Your meddling aunt's opinion is no longer the only data point. Thank goodness for that.

**Company "half truths" have been supplemented by the "whole truth."** Pre-Internet, customers' only way to learn about you was through what you provided—brochures, testimonials, and so on. Let's face it. Those materials are designed to tell only part of the story—the good part. I, for one, never included letters from dissatisfied customers with my proposals.

Now, however, the dark side of your story is readily available online through third-party and customer reviews. Anyone with the inclination can look up what everyone who cares says about you, good and bad. Somebody feel like they got ripped off? There's a scathing review online. Someone feeling burned by your lousy customer service? There's 140 characters' worth of venom on Twitter with your hashtag attached.

Your prospective mate can find out what your bitter ex really thinks of you. Moving to a new town will not help.

**Info about your solutions has been supplemented by info about you personally.** In days of yore, the customer had to wait until you showed up/called to get a feel for whether you were the kind of person they would enjoy doing business with. In modern times, they know all about you before you show up, thanks to the mechanisms we already discussed. Woe to the person who has a reputation for sharp dealing or lousy service—it's all out there.

Aunt Nellie's recommendation may have been based solely on what kind of car she saw you in. Your prospective mate now knows better. Woe to the wooer with a trail of bitter ex-lovers out there in cyberspace.

So is this Internet thing good or bad? It is neither good nor bad, grasshopper—the Internet is just a thing with no intrinsic properties like goodness or evilness. The Internet is sort of like a knife—you can use it to cut someone up, or you could use it to cut someone a slice of cheese.[18] It's how you use it that counts.

## Putting Your Best Cyberfoot Forward

We'll save the marketing and PR talk for another time. (*Love and Marketing*, anyone?) Instead, let's focus on the things you can personally control (or semicontrol) as a seller.

Start with a good LinkedIn profile. As of this writing, LinkedIn is the number-one way business professionals prequalify (learn about) you as a seller, and it looks to be that way for a while. Then again, LinkedIn may be the MySpace of business networking sites.

Plenty of experts have expounded on how to build a good LinkedIn profile, so I'll be brief.

First, basics like grammar and spelling count. That one typo says more about you than you'd like. It's incredible how some people can instantly spot a typo or grammatical error in a big, giant pile of words . . . and how much it says about your effectiveness. Some

---

18. A fine Gouda, perhaps. Although I love me some Velveeta.

of you have almost put this book down already because of the loose language, typos, and grammatical errors you've noticed so far.

Second, the company you keep matters. The more powerful, well-known, and respected your connections, the better it reflects on you. Conversely, if three-fourths of your connections are relatives and childhood pals, that is not as good. If a VP of operations, for example, is considering you and looks at your profile, it helps your cause if there are other VPs of operations in your network.

Third, focus and leverage your skills. Too many skills may put you into "jack-of-all-trades, master of none" territory, which is not great unless you aspire to be a jack-of-all-trades. And in keeping with those skills, do something proactive—share an article, post a blog, comment on something, add some value. LinkedIn is the modern, electronic way of clipping articles out of the paper and sending them to customers.

Finally, keep your shirt on. I am not kidding you—a sales rep for one of my clients had a shirtless photo of himself as his LinkedIn profile photo. A *former* sales rep, that is. In other words, keep it professional. Save the family/pets photos for Facebook.

Speaking of Facebook, you are fooling yourself if you think customers aren't checking out your Facebook page. If you're not on Facebook, that's your call, but I consider it to be another way to help customers learn more about you as a person. And last time I heard, people still buy from people.

So, here are my top few tips on how to make your Facebook profile work for you.

First, celebrate more, brag less. There's a fine line between "I'm so happy for my kid" and "Look how awesome my kid is." Celebrating: Posting an RIP homage to your old car. Bragging: Posting a picture of your shiny new car and telling people how much you paid for it. Bragging about your sales success is unseemly.

Second, make it about others, not just you. Hint: If over 50 percent of the pictures you post are selfies of no one but you, you are in narcissist territory. Even your selfies should be celebrating time with others, not just showing off your tan. (Also, too much sun is bad for you.)

Third, keep your clothes on. And the booze down. Do I have to elaborate on that one?

Fourth, manage your groups. That's just good security—Grandma and Grandpa should have a different level of visibility into your children's activities than the general public. A lot of sellers I know keep their professional and personal "friends" separate via group settings.

Finally, reconsider the profanity-laced tirade against all the idiots in the world. One of them may be a prospective customer checking you out. Positivity is attractive. Bitterness may be funny, but it's less attractive.

## Flip Side: There Are No Cold Calls

Again, the cold call has been rendered extinct by the Internet. Unless you are in a retail/consumer sale (in which case, you might be reading the wrong book), there is literally no excuse for not doing your homework on prospective customers.

In other words, you need to *know before you go*—from both a business and a personal perspective. What do I mean?

Business: Google the company.[19] Invest in a business research tool like D&B or Hoover's if your situation warrants it (for instance, you're calling on a lot of publicly traded companies). Get to know

---

19. Duh!

your industry's resources—most trade associations have online intelligence available. Check relevant hashtags on Twitter.

Personal: Google the person.[20] Look them up on Facebook, LinkedIn, and whatever other sites are cool that I have no idea even exist as I write this. Search for them on Twitter. See if they've posted recipes on Pinterest. Cruise the online dating sites to see if th . . . wait, was that the Lens of Love leaking in here? Yes, I think it was.

Let me offer just one more shout-out to my favorite online business tool—LinkedIn. It's the Rolodex that updates itself and cross-references itself! If you do nothing else, spend the time with LinkedIn to see who you know who knows people you need to know.[21, 22]

## Suck less at selling:

- Do your homework, and know for sure that customers are doing theirs.

- Make it easy for customers to learn about you.

- Replace doctored testimonials with authentic, live references.

- Use social media for drunken rants/pictures at your own peril.

---

20. Again, duh!
21. True story: On more than one occasion, I have found someone in my network who is connected to people I'm trying to get to know. Their perspective and inside intelligence has been übervaluable.
22. Another true story: I'm writing these words on a Thursday night. Friday morning, I have a call to finalize details of an engagement with a former client who got a new, bigger job at a new company, remembered nothing but my name, and looked me up on LinkedIn. I love the Internet!

# Looking for Love in All the Right Places

Assumption: You are reading this book because you do not have a steady supply of prequalified customers who call you and ask to buy. (If this does describe you, you are not in sales. You're in customer service.) Therefore, you are in the business of prospecting, and that's what we're talking about here—going out and finding business. Some say *hunting*—of course, I say *looking for love.*

But before you head out there into the wild world of prospecting (be it business or love), get it together! As always, this advice applies to both the salesperson and the lover.

**Know yourself and play to your strengths.** Your job as a prospector is to do what works for you, not what works for others. You, my friend, are a snowflake—you are unique, and you have a unique set of prospecting strengths and weaknesses. Ask (and answer) these questions to determine your optimum prospecting strategy:

- When do you have your best energy for prospecting?

- What's your stamina for prospecting? How much of it can you take at any given time?

- In what medium do you communicate best? E-mail? Phone? Tweeting? (I'm serious. Mostly.)

- Where do you feel the best about approaching the organization? At what levels and why?

Armed with the answers to these questions, create a prospecting strategy that works for you. Conversely, you'll want to avoid prospecting strategies that highlight your weaknesses. This will often mean going against the grain—your best-fit strategy might not be what everyone else in your company does. You might not fit the mold, and that's okay—as long as your reasoning is sound (and you have a reasonable boss). Let's face it—you might also have to shore up your game, because that's what it takes in your industry. Let results be your guide.

If you're a morning person who hates dancing, doesn't drink, and cooks a mean omelet, looking for love at the club might not be the best fit. Think about a networking breakfast event. Or learn to dance.

**Know what you're *not* looking for.** This is not the same as "Know what you're looking for." Here's why: It's a lot easier to disqualify prospects than qualify them, particularly early in the sales relationship. You know based on experience that if a prospect doesn't meet certain demographic criteria, it probably won't work. You can either determine a lot of that before you even approach, or you can figure it out relatively early. It takes longer to find out if there's a values match or if their needs are a fit for your solutions. So start with disqualification, and keep an open mind from there.

It's easier to figure out the showstoppers than the perfect fit. Jerks identify themselves right away. It takes longer to find out if they're your soul mate.

**Believe in yourself and the value of your offering.**
Confidence is attractive—if you believe in what you're selling,
you radiate it. You establish a business partnership. You require
reciprocal commitment. You avoid getting played because you're
not desperate. There are plenty of folks who will buy from you,
so you are not into being used and abused by prospects. You sell
with dignity and demand respect. And as a result, you end up with
better prospects and more results.

Love yourself, and you will be loved by the right people. Respect
yourself, and you will be respected. Don't give it up because
you're needy. You've gotta know, before you go any further, will
the customer love you? Will they love you forever? There is no
sleeping on it.

## Great Prospecting Starts with Strategy

I'm not here to share traditional sales crap like "Killer Opening
Lines" or "Perfecting Your Elevator Pitch" or "Twenty-One
Opening Questions That Close the Sale." We're also not having a
talk about optimizing your first impression—some of that is out of
your control.[23]

I offer no tactical advice for three reasons. First, prospecting
is about much more than first impressions—it's about having a
strategy that minimizes the import and impact of a single impression. You don't want your business success to come down to

---

23. Read *Blink* by Malcolm Gladwell for an introduction to the power of first
impressions and how it's cool to be tall like me.

whether you show up in the right color suit. Second, customers are getting wise to the fallacy of relying on first impressions. They've read the book too. They're more interested in the substance these days. Third, your approach is your business. Again, you are the mighty, unique snowflake—what works for you is what works for you. Beware somebody trying to sell you their secret prospecting sauce—it's theirs, not yours.

So, let's talk about prospecting strategy best practices. To give ourselves a Lens of Love opportunity, let's look at an old-school, and still widely employed, prospecting scenario—the nightclub! Imagine yourself out at the club, looking for love.

**Know before you go.** There is no substitute for good research and reconnaissance. See my chapter on the demise of the blind date/cold call for more detail.

Before you buy that person a drink, you may want to check them out for a minute from a safe distance.

(Mixed Metaphor Alert!) Get to know customers in their natural habitat, not the zoo. For example, at an industry convention, the trade show expo floor is a zoo. It's not an environment where people are acting naturally. If you want to meet customers (zebras) in a more relaxed environment, spring for a full admission and go to the sessions. They're more at ease in the herd, and you don't have that annoying exhibitor tag that identifies you as a predator (hyena).

Yeah, some of you met your soul mates at the club, but more of you met your soul mates at a friend's house or at work.

**Go where your competition isn't.** The trade show floor example here too: would you rather be surrounded by your competitors (other hyenas) or surrounded by prospects (juicy, succulent zebras)? Far better to be in the sessions. Outside of the conference, seek the associations and organizations that your customers frequent.

Fellas, here's a little secret about ladies' night at the club: it's mostly fellas. The club is using the promise of ladies to lure you there, and it works . . . on you and dozens of your competitors.

Example: Once upon a time, when I was still single, a couple of friends invited me to go to a casino in the middle of Minnesota. Now, I'm not a big gambler, so I wondered openly what the attraction was. "Trust me," said my friend Andrew. "It'll be worth it."

Well, the weekend we went just happened to be opening weekend of deer-hunting season, and thus . . . *it was all ladies!* Talk about a roomful of lonely women . . . let's just say, it was good hunting. For me. (Also, Rick Springfield was playing. For real.)

**Get a trusted wingman.** The only thing better than approaching prospects yourself is having a high-trust resource approach them on your behalf. Having a customer write you a testimonial letter, recommend you on LinkedIn, or call/e-mail a prospect on your behalf is way more credible than you doing it yourself. Yes, it's hard to do, and it happens rarely—that's what makes it so golden.

If you're a fella in the club trying to get to know a female, you know who your best wingman is? A wing*woman*. True story: Before we started dating, fell in love, and got married, Donna and I used to perform winghuman duties for each other. Seriously! It totally works!

Is there more? Could I regale you with tales of prospecting triumph and tragedy? Yes, I could, particularly at the club (mostly tragedy). Instead, let's wrap it up.

## Suck Less at Selling:

- Great prospecting starts before you start, with knowledge of yourself, your objectives, and what you don't want.

- Believe in yourself and your solutions, and the world is more likely to believe in them too.

- Have a strategy that differentiates you from your competition.

- Be prepared to kiss some frogs. Despite your best efforts, prospecting remains a challenging, high-effort/low-result game.

- Encounter prospects in their habitat, not yours.

# Suspect or Prospect?

L et's start this section by looking through the Lens of Love, shall we?

True story: I once knew a girl who was in love with a boy. She was in love with him because he was perfect in almost every way: smart, funny, responsible, sensitive, considerate, good fashion sense. She loved him because he was perfect for *her* in almost every way: same values, same hopes and dreams, same taste in music, food, and clothing. They were both single and looking to settle down. For a full year, they were inseparable— dinners, movies, vacations, and shopping trips.

And in the end, he left her for somebody else.

This doomed romance has a sales equivalent, of course.

You court a prospect that seems perfect in almost every way: They have a budget, you're talking to the decision maker, they fit your ideal prospect profile. They seem perfect for *you* in every way: Your sales calls have been fantastic, you made a killer presentation, they love your proposal. You have spent a ton of time making contact with all the key influencers, understanding their decision process, and spending your T&E money on them.

And in the end, they decide to . . . buy from somebody else.

If you examine a book closely, there's usually a foreshadowing of the tragic end to come. But, as is often the case in real life, the foreshadowing is not what's *in* the story, it's what's *missing*. The missing ingredient in each of these examples is what separates the prospects from the suspects.

## Definitions

**Suspect**: You suspect/hope you have an opportunity because of demographics but haven't found a compelling need to change.

**Prospect**: There is a real prospect of a deal because your demographics line up, and there's a compelling need to change.

Did you see the critical difference? Ultimately, the need, or absence of need, is the difference between a *prospect* and a *suspect*. If you're into things like the Sales Funnel, the figure on the right visually depicts what I'm talking about.

Suspects are above the sales funnel because you have not yet *qualified* whether they warrant a full-blown selling process. They're not *qualified* to be in your forecast yet.

You suspect she might be willing to go out with you, but you haven't slipped her the note (old school) or texted her yet (new school). Ask the question, tiger!

Prospects have *qualified* for your full-blown selling process because you have *qualified* them.

You asked her out, she said yes, and it's time to trim that mullet (old school), fire up a romantic Spotify playlist (new school), and go get 'em, tiger!

If the *italics* weren't making it clear enough, we're talking about *qualifying*. Of course, I have some points to make about qualifying. But keep in mind, these points are general advice (models), not specific instructions (recipes).

## Simile Alert!

Why general and not specific? Because qualifying is like cooking chili, not baking a cake. For the culinarily challenged, I will explain.

If you're baking a cake, there is usually a single right answer— the range of outcomes is finite. Ingredients, amounts, and sequence are all prescribed—you can't decide, "I like eggs, so I'll pull the cake out of the oven halfway through and add a few more eggs. And while I'm at it, I'll add some anchovies." And messing with the recipe will most likely result in failure, unless you have gone to baking school and/or spent countless hours in trial and error.

On the other hand, if you're cooking chili, there are a great number of right answers. You can add what you like, as much as you like, when you like. Anchovies? Go for it. Heck, you can even spice up that chili on its way from the bowl to your mouth. And messing with the recipe is just messing with the recipe—in fact, tinkering with the recipe often yields improvements in the result. Anyone with a rudimentary knowledge of cooking can make chili.[24]

## Qualifying with Love

### Needs before Budget

Lots of sellers believe in qualifying for budget first—"So I know I'm not wasting my time." Hey, if you want to limit your opportunities to prospects who have already established a budget, go for it. However, I ask almost every workshop if anyone has ever sold something to a prospect who started with no budget—at least a couple hands always go up.

Here's another way to look at it. Do you have a budget for replacing your roof this year? If your current one went kaput, you'd find the money, right? (Those of you who rent and thus don't have to replace "your roof" may substitute "your liver.")

The point is, if the need is strong enough, customers find the budget. And just because the need isn't strong enough when you start talking doesn't mean it won't be strong enough by the time you're done.

In fact, in some ways, I *prefer* talking with customers before they're setting aside budget, because I can influence it. Plus, once

---

24. I make a fine chili, for instance.

a budget has been set, your prospect is more likely to be talking to your competitors.

Donna was not looking to get married when we first met. And she *really* wasn't looking to marry the likes of me.

## Real Needs are Seen *and* Felt

There once was a company I was sure I was gonna do business with. Their sales were flat while the industry was growing. They had just lost a bunch of experienced salespeople and replaced them with relative newbies. Friends in the company told me their closing rates and sales cycles were abysmal. No new products in the pipeline. A call to HR confirmed they offered virtually no development for salespeople. And I sell sales training!

*Real needs = Facts + Feelings*

So, armed with all this data and evidence, I called on the VP of sales. (He took my call right away—another positive sign!) I walked in as prepared as a seller could be and, therefore, confident in my approach. Imagine my surprise when, ten minutes into the call, he said, "Not interested."

"B-but," I stammered, "I can help your salespeople close more and faster! Especially the new ones!"

His reply was delivered in that "this call is over" tone: "We're doing fine. Costs are down, so we're profitable enough. We don't need sales training." And with that, I was essentially out the door, stunned and on the street.

The point is, I could *see* the need, but the suspect wasn't *feeling* it. And until those two factors come together, you have a *potential need*, not a *real need*. And customers rarely buy things that satisfy potential needs. Even life insurance, which would seem to be an exception, exists to satisfy a real need: "I have evidence I will die someday and feel the need to make sure I leave my family in good financial shape."

She's single. She hasn't had a date in a year. All her friends are getting married. Her clock is ticking. She has a history of dating people just like you. All those facts are meaningless if she's happy on her own. Or she hates you.

The other potential need trap is when customers feel the need but cannot support it with evidence. This is a want, and unless your customers can pull the trigger on their own, your chances of success are lower.

When I was a senior in high school, I *felt* that taking my then girlfriend to a drive-in movie would profoundly improve my existence. However, without the evidence to back up my claim, I was unable to persuade the ultimate decision makers (my parents) to loan me their 1980 Chevy Caprice two-door. Too bad—that thing had a massive backseat.

**Suck Less at Selling:**

- Don't get fooled by demographics—real prospects are the ones with needs you can meet.

- Don't ask about budget until you've determined and developed needs—needs are why customers find the money.

- Cook your own chili. There is no magic qualifying recipe. These are just ingredients.

- Needs, like beauty, are in the eye of the beholder—just because the facts say it doesn't mean prospects feel it.

# *Demographics Do Not Equal Needs*

As a sales manager, I can't even count the number of conversations I've had with sales reps that went something like this:

Me: So, why is Company X a prospect?

Seller: Well, first of all, they're a huge prospect. They're not happy with the price they're getting from their current vendor. They have budget left for this year. I'm talking to the decision makers. They asked me for a proposal. I'm sure I'll close 'em this quarter.

Me (*raising eyebrow skeptically*): Oh?

Now, let's replay that conversation through the ever-handy Lens of Love:

Mom: So, why will so-and-so marry you?

Besotted suitor: Well, first of all, she's *really* hot. She's not happy with the attention she's getting at home. She's free this Saturday night. She makes her own decisions. She asked me to take her to Cancun. I'm gonna propose to her there—I'm sure she'll say yes.

Mom (*raising eyebrow skeptically*): Oh?

So would you forecast a long, happy marriage? What about your chances of taking a competitor's customer? Really? Now, before we all go ordering tuxedos or counting our commissions, let's look at the classic seller mistakes inherent in this example.

**Mistake:** Assuming your biggest companies are the prospects most worth pursuing

Fact: "A huge opportunity" does not equal "your opportunity."

Lens of Love: "That hottie is looking for love" does not equal "that hottie is looking for *your* love."

**Mistake:** Assuming problems equal needs

Fact: Dissatisfaction with current state does not equal a desire to change that state.

Lens of Love: Not everyone in a lousy marriage wants a divorce.

**Mistake:** Assuming "permission to sell" means the customer is ready to buy

Fact: Curiosity about options is different from a commitment to change. Very different.

Lens of Love: Some married folks will allow you to buy them a drink . . . because they want a free drink, not you. (Again, I am going on hearsay here.)

**Mistake:** Assuming a request to jump through hoops means there's a prize on the other side

Fact: Some customers undergo periodic reviews of the market without intending to change.

Lens of Love: "Buy me a drink?" means "I am looking for love" less often than you think. (So my friends tell me.)

In fact, any mom/sales manager worth their salt would strongly suggest this suitor/seller is deluded—they are mistaking demographics for needs. And that's a classic selling error.

So how do you avoid this classic error?

- Focus on needs as the primary determinant of your prospects. Of course size, um, matters, but it's not the primary characteristic of your best prospects.

- Focus on *why* they would change—that's the key to understanding customer needs and whether you have a real prospect instead of a mere suspect.

- Don't mistake availability for interest.

- Don't mistake your investment for their commitment.

To help clarify the situation, I've constructed the following table. The point here is to not confuse demographics with needs. This is a troublesome trap in professional selling—attractive suspects who are willing to meet with you and let you do your mating dance are not necessarily prospects.

|  | DEMOGRAPHICS | NEEDS |
|---|---|---|
| *Orientation* | Quantitative–tangibles | Qualitative–intangibles |
| *Definition* | Facts, statistics, characteristics, qualities | Feelings, opinions, attitudes, beliefs |
| *Attraction* | Make someone attractive to another | Make someone attracted to another |
| *Sales Version* | Decision maker with a lot of budget, urgent deadlines, and what looks like an opportunity to help | They want to solve a problem or take an opportunity; they want you to help |
| *Love Version* | Available, good looking, employed, right sign | Lonely, dissatisfied, seeking companionship |

Confusing demographics with needs leads to confusion and potential stalking. "Hot" and "lonely for you" are two entirely different things.

## Case Study: My Prom Career[25]

When I was a senior in high school, I went to *three* proms. That's right, three—all in a two-month period. Wasn't I studly? How lucky was I? My high school (and thus hormone-controlled) brain said, "Dan, that's three times the make-out action!"

Well, no. Only one of my three prom dates was actually interested in me—the other two were simply interested in going to prom, and I was a gullible-enough fellow not to realize it. I fell into the classic trap of mistaking demographics (cute girl my age) and availability (willing to let me take them to prom) for needs. And it turned out, they didn't need my awesome make-out skills at all, just my escort.

What did I get out of it? The opportunity to rent three tuxedos, buy three corsages (one of the wrist variety), and beg my parents for the car two extra times. As far as return on investment goes, that may not have been the most productive spring of my life. (The fact that I got 50 percent off my third corsage was not much consolation.) But for a while there, I had a full make-out pipeline!

## Suck Less at Selling:

- Don't confuse demographics with needs.

- Don't confuse demographics with needs.

- Don't confuse demographics with needs.

---

25. This is an absolutely true story. Ask my parents.

# Speed Dating at the Trade Show

I've had the pleasure (and pain) of experiencing trade shows from three perspectives.

1. As a young seller, I worked the booth. I spent many long days on unpadded floors trying to tempt passersby with my brochures, my trinkets, and my bowl of candy.

2. As a customer, I walked the trade show floor. I spent many long days on concrete floors trying to avoid salespeople while helping myself to brochures, trinkets, and fistfuls of candy.

3. As a consultant, I have been paid by my clients to evaluate their trade show performance and to compare their performance to the competition. I spent many long days on concrete floors observing the wary dance between sellers and customers (like zebras and hyenas circling the same water hole, except the hyenas have bowls of candy and trinkets).[26]

Because of these three perspectives (probably at least one more than you) and because I have experienced trade shows in at least two dozen different industries (almost certainly one more than you), I am uniquely qualified to discuss typical behaviors,

---

26. I also may have taste-tested the candy for quality-control purposes.

what works and what doesn't, and what to do about it, which is why I wrote the book, eh?

So, does the love metaphor hold up when we're talking about selling at trade shows? I think the most direct comparison is to speed dating, a relatively recent phenomenon in love but a time-honored tradition in selling.

For those of you unfamiliar with one or both, let's define the terms. (Note: I have not speed dated, but I have talked with folks who have speed dated and lived to tell the tale.)

## Trade Show

For convenience, I will use the form of trade show that's used 99 percent of the time.

**Goal:** Sellers and buyers meet as many of each other as possible in the hopes of finding a match.

**Scenario:** Sellers are arranged around the trade show floor in booths, wearing nice clothes and armed with brochures, trinkets, and candy. Sellers examine a list of trade show attendees and wait for buyers to approach their booth. They're looking forward to drinking heavily (on their company's expense account) when this thing is over. Buyers are armed with a list of exhibitors and an idea of what they want to see. They are also wearing name tags. They too are looking forward to drinking heavily (at a vendor-sponsored event) when this thing is over.

## Process:

- Buyers move through the trade show floor, stopping at each booth for a short period of time.

- Sellers and buyers engage in polite conversation, each sharing information about themselves.

- At the end of the discussion, buyers move on to the next booth, usually with some information on the seller, a trinket, and/or some candy.

- If the buyer feels the seller is qualified, they signal their interest, usually by leaving a business card in the bowl (old school) or allowing their name tag to be scanned (new school).

- If the seller feels the buyer is qualified, they signal their interest, usually in the form of making a note of whom they're going to follow up with.

- If both parties have signaled their interest, post–trade show contact is established, and things play out from there.

**Outcome:** Many sellers and customers have met each other at a trade show, fallen in love, and lived happily ever after. Many sellers and customers have walked away from a trade show thinking, *There's a day of my life I can never get back. At least there's alcohol.*

**Why It's Supposed to Work:** We fancy ourselves excellent at making judgments based on first impressions. We think we can judge a book by its cover or, in this case, a company by its trade show booth and the sellers therein.

**Why It Doesn't Always Work:** We'll get to that. But first . . .

## Speed Dating

For convenience, I will use the most common form of speed dating—boys and girls, although other forms certainly exist. Translate in your head if necessary.

**Goal:** Boys and girls meet as many of each other as possible in the hopes of finding a match.

**Scenario:** Boys are seated around the club at tables, wearing nice clothes, armed with facts about themselves, smart questions, and witty anecdotes. They are wearing name tags. Boys examine a list of girls and wait for said girls to approach their table. They're looking forward to drinking heavily when this thing is over. In fact, they may have started that process already. Girls are armed with a list of boys and an idea of what they want to see. They are also wearing name tags. They too are looking forward to drinking heavily, perhaps with drinks supplied by one or more of the boys they just met.

## Process:

- Girls rotate through the club, stopping at each boy's table for a short period of time.

- Boys and girls engage in polite conversation, each sharing information about themselves.

- At the end of the discussion, girls move on to the next table, having gained some information about that boy (and in rare cases, some candy).

- If the girl thinks the boy is a potential mate, they signal their interest, usually by marking a card and

> leaving their phone number (old school) or Twitter
> handle/IM address (new school).

- If the boy thinks the girl is a winner, they signal their
  interest in the same way.

- If both parties have signaled their interest, post-speed
  dating contact is established, and things play out
  from there.

**Outcome:** Many people have met speed dating, fallen in
love, and lived happily ever after. On the other hand, I know
people who have walked away from speed dating thinking,
*There's a night of my life I can never get back. At least there's
alcohol.*

**Why It's Supposed to Work:** We fancy ourselves excellent at
making judgments based on first impressions. We think we can
judge a book by its cover or, in this case, a potential mate based
on five minutes at the table.

## What Doesn't Work:

There are a lot of ways to suck at trade show selling. In my
experience, they boil down to these three core reasons for sucking.

**Overrehearsed.** If you've developed and polished a set of pithy
benefit statements or an "elevator pitch" about your solutions,
you are overrehearsed. The trade show is not a test of your
smoothness. In fact, too much smooth can cause prospects to
grab a piece of candy and run.

You've been funny. You've been cool with your lines. Ain't that the way love's supposed to be? No. No, it ain't.

**Feature dumping.** I am constantly amazed at how easy it is, even these days, to get sellers at a trade show to spew features and benefits all over me. Just walk up to a booth, point to something, ask, "What's up with that?" and get ready for the deluge—what they do, why they're awesome, who their biggest customers are, and so on. It's almost like sticking a finger down their throat.

If your answer to "What do you do?" includes your title, your job responsibilities, and the fact you have a company car, you are guilty of feature dumping, love-style.

**Hyperfocused on qualifying.** The opposite of feature dumping is a relentless focus on qualifying the customer. What's their title? Do they make the decisions? Are they looking to do something this year? What's their budget? Even just a little too much of that is a bad thing. You have to earn the right to qualify.

Not recommended for the speed date: "How much money do you make? Do you own your own home? How soon do you want to have children? How many?" Creepy!

**Summary:** We can sum this all up in a single term: self-centered. If you're too focused on yourself, your awesomeness, and your own needs, you're alienating potential customers.

**Summary:** If you are a self-centered speed dater, you will scare away potential mates, and you will leave with no phone numbers/IM addresses (and perhaps drunk).

## What to do instead

- Ditch the pitch. The answer to "What do you sell?" should be as simple as possible, not a litany of features and benefits. Your story should be fresh, not canned.

- Qualify for need, not authority/budget/timing. After all, if they're only there to eat your candy, it doesn't matter what their title is or whether they have budget for this year—you're not getting any.

- Break the ice by asking about the experience they're having.

- Think of trade show selling as a series of speed dates. If you wouldn't do it on a speed date, don't do it on the trade show floor. 'Nuff said.

- Get padding under that carpet! It's hard to be effective when your feet hurt.

- Enjoy alcohol in moderation. If your customers are at the post–trade show happy hour, you're still selling whether you realize it or not. Same for speed dating.

## Bonus Tip: How to Leverage Your Trade Show Investment

**Set up appointments in advance!** If you and your customers/ prospects are going to be there and you know it before you go, arrange appointments instead of hoping that when they show up, you're in the booth and not the bathroom.

**Contact prospective customers personally**, and invite them to your booth. A phone call or e-mail from you to them is more personal—and more effective—than a marketing touch or mass mailing.

**Have something to do**. Making your booth relevant and engaging with an assessment, tiny demo, or short activity/challenge beats a bowl of candy for separating true prospects from the candy hogs and trinket collectors.

**Bring customers!** Remember the LOVE LADDER: your prospective customers would much rather talk to actual customers than you. Example: I recently attended a trade show where learning technology vendors were speed dating college administrators (or trying to). The hit of the trade show floor: two vendors had students in their booth! I saw prospects completely giving salespeople the Heisman and then waiting in line to talk with the students.

**Have a technical expert at the ready**. Again, apply the LOVE LADDER—your technical folks outrank you. Even having them available remotely via WebEx, Skype, or similar is useful.

# Getting the Rose: RFPs, RFQs, and RFIs

In this section, I will attempt to equate the RFP (request for proposal) process to a morally bankrupt element of pop culture.

As I write this, another season of *The Bachelor* is set to kick off on television. If you are reading this book far in the future, hopefully a couple of things have occurred: first, this book has achieved "timeless literature" status (thus you are not reading it ironically); and second, *The Bachelor* is safely off the air and out of syndication, where it can do no further harm.

In case this is true or you've been able to avoid this bit of pop culture, let me explain the television show *The Bachelor*.[27]

**The Bachelor As Far As I Can Tell after Thirty Minutes of Research:**

1. Supereligible young man declares himself available. He is thus known as "the bachelor."

2. Selected eligible females are invited to win the young man's love and thus his hand in marriage. They are known as "the hopefuls" (my term).

3. The bachelor (or rather, the show's producers) put the hopefuls through a process of elimination to determine

---

27. I have actually watched portions of this show. For research purposes only.

the "best fit" mate for said bachelor. The process includes these elements:

- one-on-one time (known loosely as "dates")

- group time where the hopefuls sweat it out in the same room

- meeting of parents

4. The hopefuls, in an all-out attempt to win the bachelor's love, become "the desperate." They pull out all the stops:

- dressing up their, ah, offerings in the most attractive and revealing packaging

- attempting to put forth their best qualities while hiding their faults

- professing their desire for the bachelor's love loudly, repeatedly, and dramatically

- attempting to undermine the credibility of their competitors

- violating their own standards of dignity

- making questionable offers and "giving it up" if necessary to win the bachelor's love

- shedding real tears if that's what it takes

5. The hopefuls are gradually winnowed (or "down selected") to a few finalists, from which the bachelor makes his final selection. Breaking of bad news, negotiations, pleas, and bitterness ensue.

- Finally, the "winner" gets the rose, and she and her soon-to-be-no-more bachelor ride off into the figurative sunset. Ah, love!

Now, go back and reread the bullet list above using these handy substitutions:

- substitute *buyer* for *bachelor*

- substitute *sellers* for *hopefuls*

- substitute *consultants* for *producers*

- substitute *business* for *love*

I believe we've just described the typical RFP process. It's *The Bachelor* of selling situations.


## What's Wrong with This Picture?

You may be able to tell by now that I have a problem or two with both the television show and the RFP process.[28] As is my custom, I will speak of sales first and then examine my points through the Lens of Love. Away we go!


## Problem #1: The Customer Has All the Leverage

There's one of them. There are several of you. The laws of supply and demand are working against you.

---

28. My number-one problem with *The Bachelor* is what it's teaching young people about love and relationships. Don't let your children watch this show until they understand irony!

One bachelor plus many bachelorettes equals several lonely bachelorettes.

## Problem #2: The Process Is Designed to Commoditize You

Consultants and procurement would love to turn the RFP process into an apples-to-apples comparison. What often gets left out are the "oranges" that make your offering unique and your solution valuable. I am amazed at how prescriptive some of these processes are.

When you put on the formal dress, a lot of the personal style that makes you uniquely lovable is sucked out. Especially if you all show up in the same prom dress.

## Problem #3: The Spreadsheet Rules the RFP

I've worked with the consultants who advise customers on how to run a "disciplined" and "rigorous" RFP process, and I've seen how often a decision comes down to who looks best on paper—not who would really work best in life. The process itself is designed to reduce a qualitative, emotion-based decision to a quantitative, logic-based one. That's often a recipe for a suboptimal decision.

What kind of marriage would it be if you were chosen based on your measurements? (Admit it: if measurements were the criteria, many of you would not be married.)

## Problem #4: The Game Is Rigged—There Is No Such Thing as a "Fair" Process

Far more RFPs than you realize are simply there to formalize a decision that has been informally made. ("The consultant says we need three bids—prepare the RFP!") In fact, I know of very few RFP processes *ever* where each vendor received equal treatment. Somebody always has the inside track.

Here's a telltale sign that you are "column fodder": if your first hint of the opportunity is the sound of the RFP hitting your inbox, you are likely not going to win. The presumptive winner has already known of and perhaps even helped develop the RFP long before you got it.

She may be dating two of you at once, but one of you is getting more action. Responding to a rigged RFP is like wooing someone else's fiancée. Good luck with that.

## What Else Could You Be Doing?

When I rail against the RFP process (as I just have), sellers ask me, "So what do we do about it?"

My number-one answer: *don't play*! Consider how else you could be spending your time:

- Developing pre-RFP opportunities where you can bring value through your diagnosis and discovery

- Finding sole-source opportunities where customers need your uniqueness and value your differentiators

- Respectfully declining to play a game that's rigged for someone else—also known as "maintaining your dignity"

You know who *really* wins in *The Bachelor*? Every season (or so I hear), somebody is astute enough to know they're not going to win . . . and they disqualify themselves. They don't wait to get booted with all its attendant humiliation. They quit wasting their time on a deal they will never win, and in so doing, they free themselves to find their true soul mate.

## What If You Have to Play?

Let's face it. You could agree with me wholeheartedly, and then your bosses say, "We need to respond to that RFP." And so you will.

There are legitimate reasons to play:

- It may be the rare, real RFP and not an arranged marriage situation.

- You may have a real competitive advantage that can't be nullified by a spreadsheet-based process designed to suck the life out of your differentiators.

- You may have to play just to satisfy the long-term relationship requirements.

Here are my top recommendations for when you have to play but fear a commoditized, rigged process:

## Question the RFP

RFPs are a set of questions you're supposed to answer, and the instinct is to answer them. However, you can determine your real chances—and perhaps even improve them—by asking questions about the RFP itself. These are key questions include:

- How did you come to this point in the process?

- What diagnosis or discovery preceded this RFP?

- Why are you asking for what you're asking for?

- How do these criteria rank? How are they weighted?

- Why are you not asking for X? (X = underrated/unrecognized need)

You get the point, but I'll make it, anyway: asking the right questions is sometimes your only hope of differentiating your offering—through introducing or elevating criteria or maybe even through the process of asking the questions.

(Note: Don't fear the fact that your questions will be shared with all respondents—a common practice by consultants seeking to commoditize the process and create apples-to-apples responses.

Simply ask the questions that differentiate you as a consultant and let the proverbial chips fall where they may.)

You wanna know what love is? You want them to show you? Sometimes asking the provocative question is the only way to unlock the puzzle.

## Get the Inside Scoop

If you know someone in the organization who can give you the real skinny on whether the game is rigged, the true criteria, or other political considerations, by all means, leverage that relationship. (If you don't, you are probably hosed.)

Want to know if you have a real chance? Ask the best friend. It worked in high school; it works now.

## Introduce an Unanticipated Solution

Sometimes your only chance to change the game is to offer up your competitive advantage whether the customer asked for it or not. Let's face it. If the game is rigged, what do you have to lose by attempting to disrupt the game?

Here's the key: Do you have a solid reason for your unanticipated offering? Can you lead with a customer need that makes your solution compelling?

If you just know that they would find your dancing adorable and endearing, by all means, bust a move.

## Call It Like It Is

If the game is rigged and you know it, consider what you have to lose by pointing out that fact. If you have no chance to win, letting the customer know that you know it takes a lot of their leverage away—you won't be pressured into unrealistic offers or price dropping.

In love, there is tremendous dignity and power in the candid walkaway.

## Suck Less at Selling:

- Is there someplace better you could be? Focus on pre-RFP opportunities.

- Is there something more you should be asking? Focus on the questions that expose the RFP for what it is.

- Is there something else you should be offering? Focus on solutions that force customers to reconsider.

# PART
# THREE

*Try Not to Suck*

# Typical Rep Syndrome (TRS)

True story: I recently helped a salesperson prepare for a set of "first calls" with some key influencers in a major sales opportunity. When I asked about what call outcomes were possible, the rep said "of course" a presentation would be the next step. When I asked why, the rep replied, "Well, that's the way it typically happens."

Other true story: A client once asked me to help them prepare and execute a major capabilities presentation for a prospect. When we got together, the first thing they did was open up a draft PowerPoint deck and start going through it. When I asked why they were preparing a deck, the VP said, "Because that's the way these presentations always go."

Other, other true story: I once sat in the customer's shoes as three HVAC vendors vied for a million-dollar renovation project in our school district (I was a member of the school board at the time). They all had a PowerPoint deck. They had all customized it with our logo. And the first ten slides of each presentation were interchangeable to the point of indistinguishable. In other words, they were . . . typical.

And that's what we're talking about in this part—the problem with *typical* (otherwise known as the curse of Typical Rep Syndrome).

We'll get right to the clinical.

**Typical Rep Syndrome** (TRS) is a common and highly contagious sales-transmitted disease (STD) usually spread through contact with infected customers and salespeople. TRS results in completely predictable selling. Common side effects include inability to differentiate, customer disengagement, and sudden feature vomiting. Without treatment (or good luck), TRS can be fatal to sales careers.

**History**: TRS has been a fact of life in commodity or transactional sales forever. It's been a benign condition, though, because *products* were the difference, and salespeople didn't have to be.

In many of today's more complex sales, *sellers* are required to differentiate through process, consultation, and brokering of resources. That's where TRS is a limiting condition.

**How It Spreads**: TRS is highly contagious and in some cases chronic. Here's how it propagates:

First, salespeople repeat to a fault. Why? Because they mistake *correlation* (I make sales *when* I do these things) with *causation* (I make sales *because* I do these things).

Example: Once upon a time, somebody asked a customer, "What keeps you up at night?" and made a sale in that same call. Now that person asks the same question in *every single call*. ("What's keeping you up at night this week, Bob?")

Second, salespeople emulate to a fault. Now *everyone* asks, "What keeps you up at night?" I even see salespeople in my seminars "cheating" by copying questions off other teams' charts. Do you really want the same questions as everyone else? Especially since they probably aren't *causing* sales? The only people you're cheating are the customers who have to endure formulaic selling.

Finally, today's TRS behaviors become tomorrow's buying process—customers end up requiring the very behaviors they typically see. (Where to you think the RFP process came from?) Ultimately, customers grant less access and force vendors into a reactive process, doing themselves a disservice in the process.

So what to do about this silent sales killer?

## TRS Prevention and Cure: Five Easy-Seeming Steps (That Aren't Easy At All)

As usual, these are easy to understand but hard to do well. And as usual, that doesn't stop me from offering my advice.

**Start from conviction.** You know who's willing to stand against convention? Someone who believes in the value of what they're doing. Conviction begets gumption.

If you believe in yourself, you don't need cheesy one-liners ripped straight from a men's-interest magazine.

**Avoid what they brace for.** One side condition of TRS is customers who are bracing themselves for questions that *every* seller asks. I've heard a lot of witty, emasculating, and obviously well-rehearsed answers to the "up at night" question, precisely because customers have had so much practice answering it. If the customer is bracing for it, don't do it.

Example: I was once out in the field observing/coaching a newer salesperson on new-business calls. We were meeting with a veteran procurement director, and in the middle of the call (which had gone fairly well to that point), the seller asked, "So, what keeps you up at night about X?"

The prospect smiled a sharky smile, crossed his arms, and said, "The only thing that keeps me up at night is nightmares where salespeople ask me the same tired questions over and over." And with that, our sales call was all but over.

If you've seen it in a movie or read it in a magazine, so has your prospective mate. Don't go there.

**Choose disarming behaviors.** Figure out what will cause the customer to lower their shield, and then follow that path. The clearest, most shining example is the fork in the road where average sellers start presenting and great sellers keep asking. Because the path of premature presentation is so typical, the path of deeper questioning is often disarming simply by virtue of being atypical.

Another powerful example of atypical behavior is attempting to walk away or anticipating the "No" answer. "I'm not sure we're ready to go there yet" is hardly ever heard coming from the mouth of a seller.

If you really want to get 'em curious, hold up at first base. (See, kids, "rounding the bases" is where . . . never mind.)

**Ask permission to defy expectations.** I'm sure lots of people run out of my consultative selling seminars and try to completely flip their style from pushing to pulling. To me, that's sort of like . . . love. (You knew I'd get there!) If you've been Captain Conservative in the bedroom your whole marriage, you may want to do a little expectations management before you jump out of the closet with the Tarzan loincloth. (Not that I would have personal experience with that sort of thing.)

"Is it okay if we just . . .?"—one of the most powerfully under-rated questions, ever.

**Deliver on the difference.** Being atypical isn't great at first—you force customers to adjust, and change is hard. There had better be some value in it for them.

If you are an insensitive lover, the Tarzan getup and the jungle soundtrack may not pay off like you hoped. Where did you get that thing, anyway?

If you're just using a technique to soften someone up for the kill, you're not authentic. You might as well stick to your cheesy closing lines.

Ultimately, success in the last point depends on the first point. Sort of ties things up nicely, don't you think? You're welcome!

## Suck Less at Selling:
- Don't be typical.
- Avoid what customers brace for.
- Choose disarming behaviors.
- Go for the no.

# *Don't Be a Stalker!*

*Well, what am I supposed to do?*
*You won't answer my calls, you change your number.*
*I mean, I'm not gonna be ignored, Dan!*

—ALEX (GLENN CLOSE), FAMOUS STALKER
IN THE MOVIE *Fatal Attraction*

As you can tell by now, I'm a child of the '80s. And I'll tell you, this movie scared the living crap out of me, for three reasons. First, I was seeing the movie with a (soon-to-be-ex-) girlfriend who was already displaying some stalker-like tendencies. Second, we had rabbits growing up, and I like rabbits. Third, my name is Dan! She's talking to me! Aaaaaaah!

Go ahead, young ones—hit YouTube and you'll see what I'm talking about. And while you're at it, think about the sales version of stalking:

- You manage to have a brief encounter with the prospect of your dreams.

- Although the contact is relatively meaningless to your prospect, you lie awake dreaming of the possibilities.

- You update your forecast and start predicting when you'll close 'em.

- You relentlessly follow up in a pleasantly persistent way, ignoring the polite indifference you encounter.

- There's a part of *no* you just don't understand.

- Failing to reconnect, you begin to resort to ambush tactics to "catch them." You call at odd hours, just happen to be "driving by" and so on. You're not gonna be ignored, Dan!

Is this a recipe for success? It certainly isn't in love, and I would suggest it's not a recipe for success in selling, either.

**Don't be "that rep."** I admit it—I've been "that sales rep" before. The quasi stalker. Needy. Most of us have, particularly early in our careers. Deep in our minds, we know it's sort of creepy, but we do it, anyway. Why do we do this?

**People are polite** . . . **at first.** In sales, many customers are too nice to tell you to shove off . . . at first. Just like that person you like might be too polite to tell you to go pound rocks. I found this out firsthand when I made my first sales foray into the southern United States. I got a lot of first meetings (polite) but not a lot of deals.

**Our role models did it.** That veteran seller with the big paychecks? Stalker. That VP of sales with the big watch and no socks on? Did it. We tend to do what we see our role models do. That's why they're called role models.

**We don't have enough pipeline.** This is perhaps the most nefarious source of sales stalking. If you don't have enough prospects, even suspects begin to look like prospects. You feel internal pressure that distorts your view (sales goggles). Your manager is urging you to "close 'em."

She hasn't told you to hose off (yet). Nobody else will give you the time of day. You're lonely, and you have urges. Relentless pursuit seems to be how Dad won Mom's heart. What could possibly be wrong with driving by her house . . . one more time?

## Painful Example from the Author's Youth

When I was a young salesperson in my second job out of college, my manager questioned me on why it was taking so long to get a particular deal done.

"Is this really a valid opportunity?" he asked.

"Of course it is," I replied overconfidently. "I'm gonna close 'em next month."

"Oh? Let's take a look at the call notes." (This was so long ago that we proceeded to open up my Act! database.) Well, it turned out that since my last proposal (six months prior), I had made *twenty-three* calls to this prospect. All twenty-three resulted either in a voice mail (not returned) or a brief contact where the prospect assured me they were "working on it" and would be ready to buy "soon." In fact, my last nine calls had gone straight to voice mail. Is it possible my prospect had a prototype version of caller ID in 1992?

This was a suspect, not a prospect. I was stalking that suspect like a kitten stalks its shadow.

Ultimately, the root cause of sales stalking is a *seller-centric* view of the universe. Your need to close, make quota, and get paid overwhelms your thinking and blinds you to the apathy—and even antipathy—you are experiencing from customers.

And just like in love, this narcissistic view of the world results in some unsavory behaviors. Don't be a sales stalker!

## Suck Less at Selling:

- Be sensitive to what you're hearing and feeling from your prospects. Are they really into you or too polite to blow you off?

- Develop so much pipeline that the loss of one prospect doesn't ruin all your dreams.

- Learn how to take *no* for an answer.

- Ask yourself, "Is there someplace better I could be?"

- Avoid the sales version of "boiling the bunny." (Go ahead and Google "bunny boiler.")

- Have some dignity, for goodness' sake.

# Leave Your Tricks at the Door

Tricking somebody is actually a form of bullying—you're meeting your own needs at the expense of others. And in selling, just as in love, the bully ultimately sleeps alone. Weeping. Like a lovelorn kitten.

Ironically, a lot of the sales tricks I see are actually done with somewhat decent intent—"I'm not tricking the customer," you say. "I'm just trying to help them." Great, but if you're helping them in a way that's ultimately perceived as trickery, you ultimately lose. The customer's perception is their reality.

Several of the sales "tactics" you may have learned in Cheesy Seller School are actually tricks. Let's take a look at some particularly common examples.

**Tactic: Sharing Other Salespeople's Customer Stories as Your Own.** Many companies encourage their sellers to share success stories with rookies, so said rookies can go out and say things like "We worked with a customer just like you who found our blah blah blah . . ."

**Why It's a Trick:** Customers buy the sales*person* just as much and sometimes more than they buy the solution or the company offering it. This is particularly true in a complex sale with long-term relationship potential. So when you share stories that aren't your own, you're tricking the customer.

Sharing other people's success stories is like trying to fool your date into thinking it's your car, not your mom's car.

**Tactic: Sharing Only the "Benefits" and Sidestepping the Negatives.** The most classic example is the glowing testimonials—you're perfect! Everything about you is wonderful!

Admit it—you've fallen into the trap of presenting a one-sided, everything-is-great version of your solutions. After all, you're not paid to tell them what's wrong with your stuff—they'll find out on their own, eventually!

**Why It's a Trick:** You're hoping the customer will buy based on the benefits and that once they realize the defects, it's too late—they've already bought! Or maybe the defects that hampered all your other customers' results won't happen to this one! Right! This is called tricking the customer to get a deal.

Sharing only the benefits and covering up the defects is like waiting until the honeymoon to show your new spouse your neck tattoos.

**Tactic: Getting the Customer Excited about a Solution They Can't Have Yet.** This is done in the hopes they'll take an "almost" solution for now.

**Why It's a Trick:** Prematurely promoting new products and services is a version of the classic bait-and-switch trick. Baiting and switching is bad.

Baiting and switching is like proposing to someone, and when they say yes, telling them you're married now but you'll "be available in Q2." (Am I reaching here? Yes. Yes, I am.)

**Tactic: Dropping Your Price to Get a New Customer.** Then, you intend to "make it up" on future deals.

**Why It's a Trick:** This is another version of the bait-and-switch trick. Unless you disclose this to the customer up front, you're tricking them into a false expectation of value. And, as most sellers have painfully discovered, once that expectation is set, it's extremely hard to break it without risking the entire relationship. (Underrated consequence: if the customer jumps to you for the crazy low price, they'll ditch you for the same offer from the next competitor.)

Lowballing price and trying to get it back is like blowing your entire paycheck on the first dinner and thinking to yourself, "We'll go dutch from now on." Good luck with that.

In a day and age where customers are more highly trained, knowledgeable, and wary than ever, sellers employ these traditional tricks at their peril. Don't do it.

## Suck Less at Selling:

- Be candid about what you bring to the table personally—don't appropriate.

- Share a balanced, realistic view of what your solutions can and can't do. Research indicates customers trust the balanced view more than the "everything is great" view.

- Don't bait and switch.

- Offer sustainable prices right from the start. If the first deal isn't good for both of you, subsequent deals won't be, either.

# *Avoid the Cringe!*

*If I could show you something interesting today,
would you be interested?*

—CHEESY SELLERS EVERYWHERE

O f all the unfortunate side effects of Typical Rep Syndrome (TRS), perhaps the most deadly to sales results are behaviors that are so clichéd as to induce cringing on the part of the observer (me) and the customer. Prepare yourself. You may look at one or more of these and say to yourself, "Hey! I say that, and my customers don't cringe." To that I would add, "Outwardly."

Again, the problem isn't the behavior itself; it's the number of times it's been used—too many. If everybody's already doing it, customers are bracing for it, and it doesn't work nearly as well as you want it to.[29] As a matter of fact, the very fact you read it in a best-selling sales book means it's overused, and you should make up your own version of the behavior. That is precisely why my advice is usually either in the form of what *not* to do or what to generally do (e.g., ask a follow-up question)—not *how* you specifically do it (the particular question you ask).

---

29. If you skipped the previous chapter on TRS, it's time to flip back there. Or perhaps you read it but weren't really paying attention. Yes, you.

Of all the cringe-inducing behaviors you could eschew, avoid these three at all costs.

## "What keeps you up at night?"

Although the intent of this question is sometimes good (I have seen salespeople ask it in a genuine attempt to understand the customer's problems), the question itself has been overused to the point of absurdity. Typical customer responses: "Nothing," "I sleep like a baby," and uncomfortable silence.

Consider retiring this old warhorse and instead ask about needs in ways that don't involve the customer's nocturnal habits.

## "If I could . . . would you?"

This question is commonly known as the "trial close." You're testing to see if the customer will bite on your offer. So what's the problem?

First, quit being coy—if you *can* do it, why are you saying *if*? And if you can't, why are you even asking the question? Second, customers are so totally onto this one, it's ridiculous. I see them cringe at the first word, *if.*

Consider euthanizing this dinosaur and opt instead for candor about what you can do.

## "What that means to you is . . ."

This is a classic form of the benefit statement. (Remember, when I say "classic," I mean "cringe inducing.") I know, I know—you're just attempting to link your solutions to customer needs. What's wrong with that?

This time, the problem runs deeper than mere overuse. Now, you—the seller (low on my LOVE LADDER)—are telling me what something means to me. Specifically, what level of awesomeness I will achieve due to your mighty solution.

Consider flushing this turd and focusing instead on questions that challenge customers to articulate the value.

Man, it's been a while. I've been holding back for quite some time.

I can't stop it. Here it comes . . .

These behaviors are exposed for the cringe-worthy tactics they are. For effect and to make my point, we'll add a "Hey, baby" to each:

"Hey, baby, what keeps you up at night?"

"Hey, baby, if I could show you a good time, would you go out with me?"

"Hey, baby, here's what going out with me means to you . . ."

I don't know about you, but I am actually cringing.

## Suck Less at Selling:

- Come up with your own questions. Don't recycle somebody else's questions, particularly those that appear in best-selling sales books.

- Substitute "Would it be useful to . . ." for "If . . . then . . ."

- Avoid questions that contain the answer you want. Ask "What would happen to your schedule?" instead of "Wouldn't you save time?"

- Avoid the trial close. It's the number-one marker of a cheesy seller.[30]

- Let customers tell you what it means to them. Benefits, like love, are in the eye of the beholder.

---

30. To paraphrase Yoda, "Close or don't close. There is no trial close."

# Stay Outta My Pants!

*The problem with being pushy is that you sometimes push the door shut instead of open.*

—ROBERT FRIPP

Perhaps no set of sales behaviors turns customers off as much as those designed to "get into the customer's pants"—namely, their pants pocket. You know, the one with the wallet in it.

In fact, there are whole chapters of books on professional selling devoted to finding out how to get into the customer's pants.[31] Sales "gurus" throughout time have coached us on how to ask questions to "identify the ultimate decision maker," "understand the buying process," and "determine budget and time frame."

Clearly, you need to know these things—your productivity as a seller depends on it. But are your questions working for the customer?

Let's take a look at some of these in detail, using the Lens of Love, Pants Version:

---

31. This chapter, on the other hand, is about not giving the impression that their pants are your sole interest.

| CLASSIC SALES QUESTION | LENS OF LOVE TRANSLATION |
|---|---|
| "Do you make the buying decision?" | "Should I be trying to get in *your* pants?" |
| "Who is the ultimate decision maker?" | "Whose pants should I ultimately try to invade?" |
| "Who else is involved in the buying decision?" | "Who is guarding your pants?" |
| "What's your time frame for making a decision?" | "When will I be getting into your pants?" |
| "What is your decision-making process?" | "How should I go about getting into your pants?" |
| "How can I best work with your decision process?" | "How do I undo that belt?" |
| "What's your budget?" | "Whatcha got in there?" |

How are we doing? What kind of impression are you giving the customer when your questions are all about getting into their pants? The amazing thing is, many salespeople are *taught* to *lead* with these questions!

How would that go on a first or second date? Let's listen in.

"Hey, how you doin'? So, should I be trying to get into your pants? Whose pants should I ultimately be trying to invade? What does the pants-invasion process look like? Will I be getting into your pants this quarter?"

I can almost feel the sting of palm hitting cheek from here.

The fundamental problem is that these questions are basically a set of gimmes—it's all about your needs and has nothing to do with the customer's needs. This problem stems from a faulty sales assumption—that because you are selling to me, you have the right to ask about my buying structure, process, and budget. Let's be clear—you have a *need* to understand those things, but you certainly don't have the *right* to ask.

Think about it. Every one of those questions is designed to get the seller closer to their goal (the wallet) and has nothing to do with the customer's needs. Premature interest in the customer's pants usually results in the business version of getting your face slapped. Customers will shut you down, give intentionally misleading answers, and generally turn off.

## Suck Less at Selling:

- If you're not sure if it's time to be talking about their wallet, it's not time yet.

- The only one reaching for the customer's wallet should be the customer.

- Don't assume the right to talk budget, buying process, and buying structure—earn the privilege.

## Q and A: Sellers Attempt to Defend Premature Pants-Grabbing

**Q:** But Dan, if I don't find out if they have a budget right away, I could be wasting my time.

**A:** If you're a seller who's in it for the long haul, you're rarely wasting your time selling to someone without a budget *right now.*

- It's worth mentioning again that in every workshop where this comes up, I ask sellers, "How many of you have sold something to a customer who had no budget when you started selling to them?" And in every workshop, hands go up. The point is, if you create/develop strong enough needs, customers will find the budget.

- Planting the seeds of future budget is valuable to the seller who plans to be around a while. A seller who *cultivates* opportunity looks different (i.e., more trustworthy) than a seller who simply tries to *capitalize* on opportunity.

- Premature pants-grabbing now could mean you blow a real opportunity to sell something later.

# Stop Punching My Bruise!

*Behind every beautiful thing, there's some kind of pain.*

—BOB DYLAN

For as long as you've been in sales, you've been surrounded by sales books that encourage you to focus on the customer's problems. Do they have a problem? How big is it? What happens because of it? There are submarines of pain, funnels of pain, pain-oriented questioning models, pain-based selling approaches . . . so many it's painful to list them all.

So where does all this morbid fascination with customer pain and problems come from? For this, we can thank one Abraham Maslow and his hierarchy of needs. In Maslow's widely accepted model, some needs come before others—you must build the first level of the pyramid before dealing with higher levels. First come biological needs, then safety, then belonging, and so on.

In other words, if you can't get enough oxygen (level one), you're not as focused on whether you're making quota (level two), and you're certainly not thinking about what your fellow salespeople think of you (level three). It all starts with the pain.

Maslow's hierarchy has become conventional selling wisdom. Reducing risk and solving problems tends to come before capitalizing on opportunities. Avoiding pain is a stronger motivator than gaining pleasure. You would choose having that bear stop chewing your leg before you would choose closing that megadeal. Or at least I assume you would.

And you know, Maslow is right—you've seen examples of customers who couldn't even focus on the opportunity you were presenting them because they were preoccupied with other (sometimes unrelated) problems.[32]

So what have salespeople done with this knowledge? We've turned it into a pain-based, problem-oriented set of sales behaviors that "uncover the pain," "develop the implications," "twist the knife," "pour salt in the wound," and "punch the bruise." All of these have been used by salespeople to describe the technique of asking questions that force clients to realize how bad off they are. We pride ourselves in the development of a variety of pain-eliciting questions. Whole selling methodologies (e.g., SPIN selling, the Sandler pain submarine) are devoted to it.

Sounds great, right? Show up and punch the bruise, and when the customer starts crying, whip out your solution. Roll the pen! The problem is that Maslow's sequence, while it applies to *customers* (people), it doesn't apply nearly as well to *selling* (the business process).

To prove my point, check out these classic sales questions applied to approaching a potential date. For the purpose of this analogy, let's assume you are a tremendous dancer.

**You:** Hey, how you doin'? (generic opening question)

**Prospect:** I'm good.

---

32. Like the time I was at a party trying to make out with a girl who was in the early stages of, um, not feeling well.

**You:** Do you come here often? (fact-finding and qualifying)

**Prospect:** Sometimes—my friends like to come here.

**You:** So, are you lonely? (early problem question)

**Prospect:** Not particularly. I'm seeing someone.

**You:** How's your current boyfriend treating you? (probing for competitive vulnerabilities)

**Prospect:** Okay . . .

**You:** Does he take you dancing? (probing for potential problems you can solve)

**Prospect:** Not really. He's not much of a dancer. (Aha! An opening!)

**You:** Doesn't that suck for you? Isn't that a problem? (exposing the problem)

**Prospect:** Well, sort of, but he's a really nice guy.

**You:** What are the implications of this lack of dancing? (developing the problem)

**Prospect:** What?

**You:** What if your friends are all out dancing and having fun, and you're just sitting there with your boyfriend? Won't you be missing out? Won't that be frustrating? What is the effect on your psyche? (punching the bruise)

**Prospect:** Uh, I have to go tend to my cuticles.

How are you doing? On the road to glory, are you?

*But Dan*, you are saying to yourself (hopefully not out loud), *I would never use cheesy lines like that in the club. I'm way less pushy than that.* And that's exactly the point—viewed through the Lens of Love, these questions are cheesy and sleazy. They're a turnoff. It's much harder to see the fallacy of this approach in selling, because pain-based approaches have become such common practice.

And that's the way most sales methods teach you to sell. Expose symptoms of the problem. Probe for the pain. Punch the bruise.

## Have You Earned the Right?

Unfortunately, customers will only share with you to the point they trust you to do right with the information. That's particularly true if they didn't come to you for help in the first place. They won't show you the bruise if they think you're just going to punch it, not fix it.

Think about it. If you were on a first date, would you start by asking, "What was the saddest day of your life?" or "What keeps you up at night?" or "What's wrong?" When you're talking with customers, especially prospects or customers that you don't know that well, what do you think they want to talk about? I can pretty much guarantee that they don't want to start the conversation by showing you their dirty laundry.

The truth is, you must *earn the privilege* of engaging in that kind of discussion and asking the "What keeps you up at night?" questions. (Although, as we've discussed, you'll want to avoid asking that particular question.)

If you want straight answers to your pain-and-problem questions, learn what's important to them *before* you go lunging for their weaknesses. It's about earning the *privilege* of asking the deep, dark questions by first making a connection and building trust, which you do by getting to know them and finding common ground, shared values, and agendas.

## Start with Stories and Values

The way people usually start a relationship is to learn about each other slowly and organically. Each of us shares a little bit of our *story*. We talk about our dreams and aspirations, where we want to go, what we want to do. In real life, appropriate questions might be "What are you interested in?" "What do you like?" "What do you want to do more of?"[33] These kinds of questions are far more interesting and inviting to the other person. They're also more likely to determine if there is a values match. Why not in selling too?

How often do you hear people say, "We want the same things in life"? That's how real people get to know each other.

The more we want the same things out of life, and the more our agendas match, the more likely we are to connect at a higher level. This is true in dating, and it's also true in sales. Buyers trust sellers more when they sense a mutual interest and shared agenda rather than a competing agenda.

Have you ever been in a relationship where you know you've earned the privilege? You can read a change in the other person's demeanor or body language that indicates that the gate is now open. That kind of organic revealing of feelings, pain, and vulnerability is much different from the traditional sales approach. Now you're responding to feeling or a hint or sign they've given you based on your knowledge of them and intimacy with them. It's organic now. It's about people with needs relating to each other, rather than a seller trying to uncover or expose pain that the customer has chosen to keep hidden.

---

33. The same questions you use on a first date apply to a first business meeting.

## When You're the Pain

Sometimes when I try to use my probing skills on my wife or my children, I realize that their pain is my probing. I'm their pain. Smart sellers know how to tell the difference between the "It's okay to ask" reaction and the "You're bothering me" reaction.

## Beware the Needy Customer

Have you ever been on an initial date with someone who was too quick to share their pain or problems? You say, "How you doin'?" and they respond with everything that's wrong about their current relationship?

Here are some terms we often use to describe these people:

- high maintenance

- needy

- baggage laden

- bunny boiler

- (insert your own derogatory term here)

Just as you would beware of the date who comes across that way, you also want to avoid the customer who's willing to go into that kind of depth with you right away. Although it could be that you just clicked and they felt comfortable enough to open up, it may be a sign of some deeper psychological dysfunction. Healthy people don't typically start conversations by airing their dirty laundry.

But in selling, you wonder, isn't it good if the customer shares their needs from the outset? Maybe it is. But if they are coming on to you that way, chances are you're not the only one getting the heart-to-heart talk. You end up with a broken heart (and a broken forecast) because you think you're the only one with the unique and special bond, when in fact they are having that same conversation with your competitors.

Ultimately, getting to the pain should be the result of a conversation that yields a connection, not the object of premature probing by the seller.

## Suck Less at Selling:

- Start with your stories and ask about theirs.

- Understand their values and aspirations before you go poking at the pain.

- Earn the right and develop the connection necessary to discuss their distress.

- Be wary of customers who volunteer their problems too soon.

# PART
# FOUR

*Love and Marriage*

# *Interesting Is in the Eye of the Beholder*

## Don't Be a Dullard

Have you ever found yourself saying stuff that you found totally interesting but left your listener totally cold? I'm pretty sure that's happened to me and you already . . . perhaps on this very page.

Has anyone every bored you to near tears with their long-winded stories of things they were totally into, but you couldn't care less about? Has that happened in this book too? I suppose it has. (Sigh.)

As a matter of fact, that reminds me of this one time when . . . hold on, was I about to do it again? That depends on two things. We'll get there after I tell you a story about the old days . . .

In the old days, people used to bore you with slide shows or eight-millimeter movies—later, VHS tapes—of their boring journeys to whatever boring place they'd been and the boring things they did while they were there being dull. Even the interminable time it took them to set up the screen/projector was boring. The Internet has sped things up quite a bit. Now you can be instantaneously bored with the Instagrams, tweets, and Facebook posts that clutter up your social media life. (Advantage: Internet.)

Same thing in business. In the days before the Internet, customers used to have to invite you in and endure an entire presentation's worth of potentially being bored, in the hopes of getting to things they cared about. In today's modern cyberworld, customers can fast-forward through the videos on your website, skim a white paper, and cruise through your online brochure. (Again, advantage: Internet.)

Painfully boring, awkward first dates involving entire dinners have given way to painfully boring, awkward online chatting.

Regardless of the speed and duration, dull persists, and boredom is persistent. Let's define what we mean by dull and boring and then talk about sources and remedies.

**dull** [duhl]
adjective, dull·er, dull·est.
1. not sharp; blunt: *a dull knife.*

2. causing boredom; tedious; uninteresting: *a dull sermon.*

3. not lively or spirited; listless.

4. not bright, intense, or clear; dim: *a dull day; a dull sound.*

5. having very little depth of color; lacking in richness or intensity of color.

Interestingly enough, every sense of *dull* mentioned in the Dictionary.com entry above can be applied to a conversation, a presentation, or a person.

**bor**·ing \bor-iŋ\
adjective
1.   dull and uninteresting : causing boredom

Examples of *boring* [I couldn't have made this up—it's straight from Merriam-Webster.com. Seriously.]
- I find her books totally *boring*. [Notice how this utterly defeats my now obviously outdated grammar.]

- I wish this book weren't so *boring*; I keep falling asleep whenever I try to read it.

What makes something—or somebody—boring or dull? Boring and dull are not innate or intrinsic properties. I have proof.

Some customers are turned on by certain capabilities of your solutions, while other customers simply do not care about those very same capabilities.

That snail collector you went out with that one time? The time where you were so bored you fell asleep *during dinner?* He's happily married now. (Still collects snails.)

In other words, *boring is in the eye of the beholder.* There's a corollary: *interesting is in the eye of the customer.* That's simple—so simple I hesitated to write it for fear of insulting your intelligence. But if it's so simple, why do sellers (not you, but someone you know) mess it up so often?

## Top Four Ways Sellers Bore Customers:

**Way #1:** Sellers *assume* that what makes up their "value proposition" must be communicated to the customer—whether they care or not. Hint: If they don't care, you are boring them.

**Example:** How many times in your selling career has the company you work for given you a PowerPoint presentation where one of the first slides is devoted to your "value proposition"? Have you ever noticed the look on your prospects' faces as you go over that slide? Are they totally engaged and into it? Better yet, have you ever skimmed or ditched the slide and felt secretly good about it?

Just because you think your snail collection is what makes you great, it doesn't mean your potential mate will see it the same way.

**Way #2:** Sellers *assume* that customers are the same and that the reason a previous customer bought from you is the reason your next customer will buy from you.

**Example:** Have you ever shared a customer example or case study and gained zero traction from it? Worse, have customers ever dismissed the case study because their business is different?

In my part-time job as a member of my local school board, we were once considering hiring a company for a million-dollar mechanical upgrade to the lone elementary school in our tiny, 1,300-student, semirural district. One potential vendor, to establish their ability to do our job, emphasized the fact they just won the largest government project ever. In Dubai. (Reminder: We are a tiny school district. In Wisconsin.) Did this story really create the feeling that the vendor was right for us? Hint: Customers are unique like snowflakes.

Just because your ex loved you for your snail collection doesn't mean your prospective mate will love you for it.

**Way #3:** Sellers *assume* they're required to conform to sales conventions like sharing a bunch of boring background information about their company before they get to interesting stuff like the customer's actual needs. (I'll explain this more in the "Nice Deck" chapter.) Hint: Just because everyone does it that way doesn't mean you have to . . . particularly if it's boring.

**Example:** Have you ever counted the number of "all about me" slides at the beginning of your PowerPoint presentation? And how similar it is to the PowerPoint presentations your competitors are probably showing the prospect?

Just because everyone at speed dating night starts by sharing something about themselves doesn't mean you have to lead with the snails.

**Way #4:** Sellers *fail* to understand what's interesting to the customer and are left to guess. Sometimes they guess wrong. Hint: There is no substitute for good diagnosis, discovery, and needs assessment.

**Example:** What percent of the introductory slides or talking points in your presentations change based on the needs of the customer you're talking to?

If you don't know how your prospective mate feels about snails, you're going into your presentation blind.[34]

## How to Stay Out of the Boring Zone

The diagram below spells it out visually, but I'm not going to let that stop me from spelling it out, anyway.

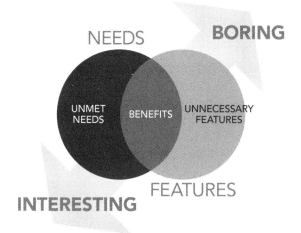

**Lead with the need.** Start by understanding the customer's needs. Done well, diagnosis and discovery are more interesting than your presentation. Good needs assessment also makes your presentation more interesting, because it allows you to . . .

---

34. This is not meant as a commentary on your snail collection. Snails are neither good nor bad. They just *are*.

**Focus on the connections between their needs and your solutions.** The interesting stuff about what you sell is the stuff that helps customers meet their needs. That's what customers call benefits, and that's what they want to talk about. Anything of yours that doesn't meet their needs is boring. So . . .

**Beware of unmet needs.** If the customer has needs that you can't meet, you are vulnerable to competitive options. This is particularly true when the customer's primary need is one you can't meet.

**Avoid unnecessary features.** If they don't see the need for it, seek to avoid presenting it. Offering things the customer doesn't need bores them at best and at worst creates objections and price concerns.

This last point is particularly important. Sharing unnecessary capabilities risks a raft of unintended consequences you won't enjoy. What's that? You want an example? You want to examine this through the Lens of Love?

I once dated a young lady with whom I was hoping to take it to the next level. She was complaining about burnout at work. "I just need to get away for a few days," she said.

So I suggested a trip to the North Shore of Minnesota. Rustic cabin? Check. Beautiful scenery? Check. Walleye and wine? Check. (I was by this time starting to visualize the romantic possibilities.)

"Fantastic," I said. "I'll set it up. I know the owners—we can all grill out. This place has kayaks we can rent and—"

"Hold up," she interrupted. "I just want to chill out for a few days. I don't need an adventure. I think I'll just hang out at home this weekend. Alone." And just like that, my romantic weekend was toast. Why? I'll tell you why:

155

- Unnecessary features introduced objections.

- Her true need (quiet) was unmet by my solution.

- The opportunity cost of losing a quiet weekend at home outweighed the benefits of my proposal.

Moral: Casanova, I am not. And, of course, lead with the need!

## Suck Less at Selling:

- Focus on the customer's definition of interesting—stuff that meets their needs.

- Use the customer's perception of value as the basis for your sales presentations—not yours.

- Lead with the need to ensure you are in the interesting zone.

- Avoid presenting unnecessary features, no matter how cool you think they are.

## Superabbreviated Q and A

Q: But Dan, sometimes I show customers things that they're not asking for, and it sparks a need—they realize they need it.

A: I hate to break it to you,[35] but you're not sparking a need; you're stumbling on a need. A need you could have understood in discovery/diagnosis, so you didn't have to rely on

---

35. That's just an expression. I enjoy breaking it to you.

luck. As they say in the backyard, even the blindfolded squirrel occasionally finds the nut. The trick is getting the tiny squirrel blindfold to stay on.

# *Shut Up and Listen*

*When people talk, listen completely.*
*Most people never listen.*

—ERNEST HEMINGWAY

*Most people do not listen with the intent to understand;*
*they listen with the intent to reply.*

—STEPHEN R. COVEY

Here's the deal: salespeople don't listen. In fact, salespeople are notorious for not listening. You know the saying "You have two ears and one mouth—use them proportionately"? That was *not* first uttered by a seller. In fact, every sales trainer in the world has said those words at some point . . . but sellers aren't listening.

Why don't sellers listen enough? I believe the number-one reason is sales opportunity. It's easy to listen when customers are talking about things that don't affect your paycheck. But the minute a need pops out of their mouths, we start:

- Thinking about how we can help

- Thinking about what we can sell

- Calculating our commission

- Plotting our next move—often a statement or some kind of closing behavior

Sometimes it's a failure of intent: you don't actually care about what the customer is telling you. (We've all been there.) And sometimes it's simply a failure of behavior.

Am I cynical? No, I'm just a guy who has seen it over and over and over again. So who's not listening? The answer is not necessarily what you'd expect.

## The Experience Trap

In my travels with salespeople, I've noticed an interesting phenomenon: experience and listening are inversely related. In other words, the more experienced the seller, the less listening occurs.

$$Listening = \frac{1}{Experience}$$

Think about it. When you're young or inexperienced, you're in learning mode. You don't necessarily know how to solve the customer's problems or meet their needs—you're just hanging in there for dear life, hoping to make it to the next step. (Or was that just me?) Listening is all you've got. So you do a lot of it—customers are educating you.

But somewhere in your sales career, the switch flips. You've seen enough customers and done enough deals where you *know*. You know exactly how you can help, what solutions will meet their needs, and how you make a sale and get paid. Sometimes you know it even before the customer does. And that's when the listening stops.

So what makes for good listening? Let's start with what doesn't.

## The Three Most Overused Listening Behaviors (or Fake Listening Behaviors)

### Claiming to Hear What They're Saying

Whenever I hear a seller say, "What I hear you saying is . . .," I cringe. I cringe because 95 percent of the time, what follows is either parroting the customer's exact words or attempting to paraphrase and getting it wrong. And customers cringe. I've seen a lot of customer eye-rolling at the first sign of this tired phrase, because you don't appear to be listening. If I were to try this at home, Donna would shut me down in a heartbeat—"Smaida, get that sales crap out of here."[36]

### Example:

Customer: "We're investigating our options because our current process relies on manual operations, and we think that we could speed things up considerably if we automated."

Seller: "What I hear you saying is, you'd like to automate to speed things up and reduce your reliance on manual processes."

Customer: "Yes."

*But Dan*, you're thinking, *what's wrong with that? Didn't I just confirm my understanding and prove that I was listening?*

---

36. Actual quote. Used with permission.

Perhaps you did, but the way you did it was (a) clichéd—everyone uses the "What I hear you saying" phrase; and (b) low level—you basically repeated the customer's words back to them.

What was missing? Two things. First, there's no evidence that you *understand*—you could repeat the words but not get what the customer's saying. Second, there's no progression in the conversation—you're treading water, not moving forward.

Instead, consider the follow-up question that both proves your understanding and moves things forward. Examples: "What kind of acceleration are you looking for from automation?" or "How much of a bottleneck are the current manual operations?" or even "Tell me more about what you mean."

Another option is to offer an interpretation—"It sounds like you're ..."

Of course, your technique will vary. But notice how these response options both display listening and move things forward. And they're not clichéd. (Yet.)

## Claiming to Understand Exactly What They Feel

Ooh, and then after you're done "hearing what I'm saying," why don't you tell me you "understand exactly what I feel," "totally get what I'm saying," or "feel my pain." That shows what a deep listener you are, right?

Wrong. All it shows is that you a) have mastered some traditional sales clichés and/or b) overestimate your ability to empathize. And that kind of overestimating turns customers off, especially when they've heard it countless times before from salespeople who don't appear to be listening.

## Following with an Unrelated Question

Third on the list of ersatz "listening" behaviors is the unrelated question. The customer answers your question, and the next question out of your mouth is either the next one on your qualifying checklist or a transparent attempt to qualify for your sales opportunity ("And are you the decision maker on that?"). If your next question is unrelated to their last answer, you don't appear to be listening.

Notice I say, "Don't appear to be listening." You may be doing your absolute best to listen, and you may be doing a good job. These behaviors, because they are salesy, typical behaviors (symptoms of Typical Rep Syndrome), undermine your efforts and make you look like all the sleazy, cheesy sellers out there who just give lip service to the ears part.

## The Foundation of True Listening

There are two ingredients that, like flour and butter in a cake, form the foundation of good listening.

1.  **Intent.** Let's face it. If your intent is to make your point, be clear, or make yourself understood, you're not listening. The opposite: truly wanting to understand where the customer is coming from.

2.  **Empathy.** If you don't care about what the customer is going through, you're not listening. You're simply waiting to make your point. That's too bad, because empathy opens the door to deeper relationships and more trust from customers.

## The Three Most Powerful (and Underrated) Listening Behaviors

These behaviors are the exception. Because they help you connect with the deep human need to be understood by other humans, these behaviors will never become clichéd. Use them as much as you reasonably can. Nobody else seems to be doing much with them.

**The pause.** This behavior is so simple and yet so hard. When the customer finishes talking . . . stop.

Pause.

Take a breath. Allow what they said to sink in.

There is no more powerful listening behavior than simply taking the time to actually listen and process. In some cases, you'll find the customer adds something to what they just said. Why? Because they feel like you're listening, and they feel comfortable sharing more. (Too long a pause, though, and they might think you're slow and try to rephrase in simpler terms.)

Finishing each other's sentences is only cute and adorable when you're not trying to push an agenda. Then it's just annoying. Try the opposite and watch your honey feel loved.

**The note.** When you write it down, you are demonstrating that you're listening, you take it seriously, and you want to remember. Taking notes shows that you're focused on the customer's data first and your sales opportunity second. Unless of course you're writing down what you're going to say next.

I take notes all the time and see the power. Even on the phone, I tell people I'm taking a note—which explains both the pause and the sounds of furious keyboard pounding (I'm a heavy typist). Side benefit: Taking notes buys you time and helps you figure out what to do next.

When Donna tells me she needs some groceries, I grab the pen and special grocery list notepad. And she would have it no other way. (Related issue: I am incapable of retaining more than three grocery items in my mind.)

**The follow-up question.** The antithesis of the unrelated question, the follow-up question delves more deeply into what the customer just told you. It attempts to clarify what you just heard. It seeks to understand the deeper meaning, root causes, or effects of an issue. And it's so powerfully simple, it's almost silly to list some examples, but here they are:

- What do you mean?

- Can you tell me more about that?

- Why?

- How so?

- Mmmm? (raise one eyebrow if you can)

This is particularly useful when you get one of those answers that invites the next question.

**You:** "Honey, are you okay?"

**Honey:** "I'm fine."

**Wrong answer**: "How 'bout some pizza?"

**Right answer**: "Fine?"

As usual, the Lens of Love makes the point for me. This is almost too easy.

## Suck Less at Selling:

- Listening starts with caring about the customer and wanting to listen.

- Don't undo good listening with bad behaviors.

- Listening takes time. Pause and give it time.

- Care enough to write it down.

- Questions are the friend of listening. Statements are often not.

# Nice Deck

*Excuse me while I whip this out.*

—Sheriff Bart, *Blazing Saddles*

As of this writing, "making the presentation" is a key component of almost every sales process. You strive for it. Customers require it (or at least endure it). And the coin of the realm, the language of the land, is the PowerPoint slide deck. Whether this is awesome or not is your judgment—it just is.

The presentation typically signifies a major milestone in the sales process, however it occurs. Here are three likely scenarios. As is my custom, I'll show a business example, and we'll look at that example through the Lens of Love. For purposes of this discussion, I'll lay them out side by side for easy comparison.

| SALES PRESENTATION SCENARIO | LENS OF LOVE EQUIVALENT |
| --- | --- |
| *Scenario #1* | |
| You receive a request for information (RFI) and are invited to make an initial presentation in advance of the sales opportunity. | You get an IM (instant message, old folks!) from the prospective mate asking why they should consider dating you. |

| SALES PRESENTATION SCENARIO | LENS OF LOVE EQUIVALENT |
|---|---|
| *Scenario #2* | |
| You receive a request for proposal (RFP), complete with specifications and requirements. You submit your proposal and are invited to present your proposal. | Prospective mate e-mails you a list of requirements for dating. You respond that you're willing to meet those conditions and are invited over to elaborate. |
| *Scenario #3* | |
| You contact the prospective customer offering an initial capabilities presentation, and your offer is accepted. | You IM the prospective mate, offering to share some reasons why you would be an excellent mate, and your offer is accepted. |
| *Scenario #4* | |
| At the conclusion of your needs analysis with the customer, you offer a solutions presentation for them, their team, and their bosses. | At the conclusion of your date, you offer to come over and tell your prospective mate, their friends, and their parents why you would be a good match. |

How we doin' so far? Are you feeling a little uncomfortable about the whole presentation-through-the-Lens-of-Love thing? Well, that's the point. Each of these scenarios should make you slightly itchy.

What do these scenarios all have in common? They all involve presenting to people you don't know, haven't met, and don't understand. They all involve your putting your best foot forward based on incomplete information. For these reasons, they all present both risk and reward for you, the seller/suitor.

Regardless, this is the dance you have to dance, so let's go for it!

## Getting Ready for the Big Presentation

Regardless of the scenario, most sellers kick it into overdrive the moment one of these opportunities becomes available. You got a date!

What do most sellers (not you, I'm sure) do when they get the opportunity to present?

- Gather the team to get input and strategize

- Spend a lot of time deciding what slides will go in the deck

- Invest in "customizing" the deck with customer logos, colors, etc.

- Rehearse and conduct "dry runs" of the presentation

- Bring along as many senior executives and technical SMEs as they can get away with

Do you know where I'm going with this? That's right, the Lens of Love!

## Getting Ready for the Big Date

Most seekers of love (my younger self included), when presented with this big date opportunity, kick it into overdrive. But is this what you would do?

169

- Gather your friends and parents to discuss your strategy for the date

- Spend a lot of time thinking about your lines

- Go out and buy a suit/dress in the prospective mate's favorite color and brand

- Spend time in front of the mirror practicing your lines and that cute thing you do with your hair

- Bring as many friends as you can get away with—plus your mom

When you look at the Lens of Love equivalent, I hope you have thoughts like "trying too hard," "going overboard," and "awkward." Maybe even "creepy." (Exception: You're going to the prom and color coordination is important.)

## The Problem with Presentations

I'll tell you what's rare. You go into a sales presentation knowing everything you need to know about everyone who will be there, the dynamics between/among them, and your real chances of a deal. Many sales presentations are not much better than a blind date.

In fact, sellers *and* customers typically use the sales presentation to expose you to more of each other—you bring more folks, and they bring more folks. The result is you're most likely presenting solutions to people you haven't met, accompanied by people they haven't met.

Add the fact that *everybody* does sales presentations essentially the same way and you are headed down the road of commoditization. Your presentation looks like every other presentation, your solution is undifferentiated, and price becomes the deciding factor. That's only good if you're prepared to win and keep the deal by offering the lowest price.

## Traditional (and Potentially Faulty) Presentation Assumptions

I'm sure YOU don't make these assumptions, but I work with a ton of sellers and sales leaders, and these assumptions are so pervasive as to be almost universal:

- Presentations are all about telling. You're paid to go in there and talk about your company, your history, your capabilities, and why your solutions would be a great fit for the customer.

- The customer is asking for it. They expect you to show up with a deck and your people. That's customary, and that's just the way business is done.

- Size matters. The bigger your résumé, client list, and team are, the more impressed the customer is.

To examine whether these assumptions hold water, let's use a special new tool: the Lens of Love, Blind Date Edition!

## Blind Date Edition

- Blind dates are all about telling. Your job is to go in there and tell the prospective mate all about you, your history, your capabilities, and why you'd be a great fit for them.

- The prospective mate is asking for it. They expect you to show up with your résumé and pictures of your pad. That's customary, and that's just the way blind dates are done.

- Size matters. I'm not going to even, ah, touch this one. Why don't you take it from here?

## Whipping It Out

Overreliance on the PowerPoint deck is one of the great tragedies of modern selling.

What do I mean by overreliance on the deck? Tell me if any of these apply to sales presentations in which you've participated:

- The title slide is up on the screen as the presentation starts.

- A printed version of the slides you're about to see is handed out. There are many pages.

- The deck drives the presentation—the seller clicks the slide, discusses what's on the slide, repeats.

- The seller reads the slides, and then adds "color" and more words verbally.

- There are just too many damn slides.

## The Average Deck

Again, I wouldn't put this stuff in here if I hadn't seen it time and time again. If you say you have never come into a presentation armed with these slides, you are most likely fooling yourself.

Slide 1: Agenda!

Slide 2: Look who I brought with me!

Slide 3: We're the leader in X! First, best, and only! (value proposition)

Slide 4: We've been around forever! (short history of how you were founded)

Slide 5: We're huge!

Slide 6: We're everywhere! (map of the country/continent/world with dots on it)

Slide 7: Look at all our clients! (logos of easily recognizable companies, some of whom you did business with once, several years ago)

Slide 8: Look at all our people! (group picture of support team/ org chart of service organization)

Slides 9 through infinity: Check out our awesome solution!

By now, you are probably already examining these slides through the Lens of Love, but I can't help doing it for you too. It makes me laugh.

## Blind Date Edition

You show up at restaurant with your mom and your best friend. As you're being seated, you ask the host for a table with a screen and projector. You're seated, and you spend the first few minutes "setting up your technology." Your best friend hands out printed versions of your slides while your mom makes small talk (fortunately, they brought their mom too).

Then the date starts. You show the welcome slide (Slide 1, with your prospective mate's photo on it) and thank them for the opportunity to present your qualifications for spending your lives together. Here come your talking points:

Slide 2: "This is my mom, and this is my best friend. We're going to talk about why we are a great fit for you!"

Slide 3: "I'm awesome at making you happy!"

Slide 4: "I've been dating for a long time—I'm very experienced!" (summary of dating history starting in junior high; mom nodding)

Slide 5: "I'm the best!" (best friend nodding emphatically)

Slide 6: "I've dated people all over this town!" (map of town with dots on it)

Slide 7: "I've dated many of the hottest people in town!" (pictures of previous dates, including that one date you had in high school with that now-famous person)

Slide 8: "I've got a ton of friends!" (picture of you and all your friends)

Slides 9 through eternity: "Check out my awesomeness!" (pictures of your car, your pad, your stereo, and so on ad infinitum or ad nauseam, whichever you prefer)

## Customers Are Not Looking Forward to Seeing Your Deck

I love how traditional sales behaviors start to look ridiculous when viewed through the Lens of Love. And that's exactly how a lot of this stuff looks to your customers—ridiculous.

Many a customer has come to curse Microsoft for even inventing this torture inflictor. You want proof? Check out all the ways I've heard customers refer to sales presentations administered via PowerPoint:

- "Death by PowerPoint"

- "Slide-Whipping"

- "Deckicide"

- "Oh My God—Another Freaking PowerPoint"

You can also tell by their behavior in the presentation. They sigh when they see all the pages. They start flipping through your handout to see how much they'll have to endure. They search (too often fruitlessly) for something that might actually be interesting/ of value to them. They tune out and disengage at various points, typically the points that are all about you and your awesomeness.

All in all, that's a pretty bleak picture, wouldn't you say? So what do you do about it?

## The Counterintuitive Sales Presentation: Ten Ways to Differentiate Yourself and Your Solution

I'll admit these suggestions take a moment to wrap your head around. Some of them seem quite radical. You will instinctively object to them because . . . well, because they're counterintuitive! That's the point!

1. *Question whether it's time for a presentation at all.* Do you know enough about the players, their needs, the dynamics among them, and what will make it an effective presentation? Are you sure? If not, consider challenging the very idea of a presentation.

2. *Leave your people at home.* Is it really necessary to bring all those people? Are you bringing them for the customer's reasons? Is the presentation doomed to fail if they are not among those present? If not, consider going solo and avoiding the "too many sellers" syndrome.

3. *Check your deck at the door.* Does the PowerPoint slide deck really meet the customer's needs? Does it differentiate you? Would you bet your commission on that? If not, consider doing away with the deck altogether.

4. *Leave your deck behind.* Are your slides engaging? Are they necessary for a robust discussion of the customer's needs and priorities and whether you match? Is that a fact? If not, consider using the deck as a leave-behind at the end of the presentation.

5. *Start with questions, not slides.* Do you really want to lead off with statements about you? Are you ready to launch into your spiel in front of people you barely know? Is that the wisest possible course? If not, consider blacking your screen and first engaging in more conversation about what they want to see and why.

6.  *Start with a customer-centered agenda.* Do you want to start by focusing on you and your awesomeness? Is it appropriate to lead with your features and not their needs? Seriously? Even after all you've learned through the Lens of Love? If not, make your first slides about them, their needs, and their desired outcomes (see the section on the customer-centered agenda).

7.  *Have customers validate and prioritize what they want to see from you.* Do you know which parts of your awesomeness matter most and to whom? Can you rank your capabilities the way your customers would? Are you quite certain? If not, consider asking the customer to rank and discuss what they want to see from you and why.

8.  *Leave your demographics for the end (if at all).* Does the customer really want to hear all about the other companies you've helped? Is the map with the dots really helping you? Honestly? If not, consider making those the last slides in your deck, the reference/background section.

9.  *Don't show them stuff they haven't asked for.* Are they telling you they want to hear how your company was founded? Do they really see value in every single feature in your solution? Really? If not, consider shutting up about that stuff and focusing on what they *do* want to see.

10. *Get a reaction as you go, not just at the end.* Are you certain the customer is picking up what you're putting down? Are you sure they see the connection between your capabilities and your needs? Absolutely,

unequivocally? If not, ask for a reaction *as you go* so you can adjust on the fly if necessary.

Again, these are counterintuitive. You should be arguing with at least some of them. Pick which ones fit your situation and your risk tolerance, try them out, and check out the results. In my experience, the more of these tactics you employ, the more customer-friendly your presentation becomes. And the more differentiated you and your solution become!

## Suck Less at Selling:

- Please reread the previous list.

- Leave traditional PowerPoint-based presentations behind.

## Q and A

**Q:** But Dan, customers expect me to go through all those things you say to avoid—how big we are, our experience, and so on. Aren't I failing if I don't meet their expectation?

**A:** Unless you hear explicitly from the customer that they'd like you to begin your presentation with your demographics, you are *assuming* the expectation. Don't do that. Validate what they want to see and why, and include/exclude demographics appropriately.

**Q:** But Dan, my VP of sales has to be there to show the corporate love. My technical people need to be there to answer the customer's questions. How can I avoid, as you put it, bringing my parents to the blind date?

**A:** Sometimes you simply can't avoid it for internal political reasons. Your best shot at doing so is the customer. If they're not requesting all those people or if they want a limited group size, you have a legitimate reason to tell your boss to stay home. Good luck with that one.

**Q:** But Dan, it's not a blind date. I already know a lot about the customer, either through their RFP or through needs assessment and qualification. What do you say about that, trainer boy?

**A:** No matter what you learned from your contact, if there are new people in the room, it's best to proceed as if you're on a blind date with them. Just like you can know a ton about your prospective mate, but meeting the parents is essentially a blind date with said parents. Plus, the average RFP/RFI is not complete. If you think you know enough to present just from the document, you are either lying to yourself or you wrote it for the customer. The former is bad; the latter is good.

# Double-Dating for Fun and Profit

I'm excited about this chapter—unlike speed dating or competing on *The Bachelor*, I have done a lot of double-dating, in both love and business! Oh, yes!

**Definition**: Double-dating is when you and your date go out with a friend and their date. To be clear, you and your friend are each on a date; you're just dating simultaneously in the presence of each other.

The most common sales version of double-dating is when you and your customer both bring a technical person to your next meeting. Hey, I'll show you my engineer if you show me yours!

## Why Sellers Go for the Double Date

As a seller, you're trying to create a more robust relationship between your company and the customer's company by introducing people to each other. Deepening the ties, as it were.

You're going out on a date with other people because it will add to the fun.

Of course you're trying to understand the customer more deeply and help the customer understand your company more deeply.

You are counting on your friend to tell stories of your awesomeness.

And ultimately, you're trying to make a sale.

You're trying to make a sale.

## What Double-Dating Is Not

Double-dating is not you and your boss/engineer/friend all trying to date the same person at once. Even in cultures where it's permissible, it's more complex, more work, and more likely to be weird. Also, double-dating is not delegating the act of dating to your companion.

## Criteria for Success: Is It Time Yet?

One of the themes of this section is about paying attention to timing. There's a lot of premature activity going on in professional selling, and bringing others in is one of the areas that's prone to prematureness. So let's talk about whether it's truly time to involve others in your sale.

- Do you have enough of a relationship already? If not, you are vulnerable to more than one of the awkward moments below.

- Do you have a strong reason for involving others? If not, you are again in awkward moment territory.

- Do you have reciprocal commitment from the customer? If not, you are dealing with Awkward Moment #1.

## Awkward Moments in Double-Dating

**Awkward Moment #1: You and your friend attempt to double date the same person.** This is awkward because it's extremely difficult to "share" either a business meeting or a date. Either one of you takes a backseat (literally or figuratively) or you end up competing for the attention of the customer. And there's nothing like your boss sticking their head into the front seat just as you're about to . . .

**Example:** I once went on a double date where my date didn't show. I wanted to see the movie, so I tagged along. Let's just say my presence as the third wheel did not improve the overall quality of my friend's date. (Sorry, Dave.)

**Awkward Moment #2: The other date does not go well.** This is awkward because if you arranged the meeting, you're responsible for the results. Plus, when your technical or executive people don't hit it off, it inevitably affects the quality of your overall meeting.

Icy relations in the backseat put a chill on the entire car.

**Example:** I once went on a double date road trip with a couple who were on the verge of not being a couple. My date and I ended up spending more time trying to avoid the bickering than we did having fun. (You know who I'm talking about, Josh and Amy.)

LOVE AND SELLING

**Awkward Moment #3: The other date goes much better than yours.** This is awkward because you and your date become self-conscious of the fact that your relations aren't nearly as warm. It's sort of a bummer.

Too much heat in the backseat steams up the car and makes your tepid front-seat relations seem lame in comparison.

**Example:** I once went on a double date with a couple who, I would guess from the noise, were intent on rounding the bases right in the backseat of my (parents') car. That was indeed awkward. And steamy. (John and Carrie, you were definitely in "get a room" territory.)[37]

**Awkward Moment #4: Your friend unintentionally undermines your credibility.** This is awkward because there are good times and bad times to reveal your shortcomings, expose your flaws, and be candid about your weaknesses. If you don't have enough credibility, those are relationship-killers, not endearing anecdotes. Sellers typically complain, for instance, that engineers "overshare."

Your friend shares amusing anecdotes about how you wet the bed or secretly adore a particularly annoying boy band.[38]

**Example:** I would never, ever double date with either of my sisters. Nothing personal, ladies; you just know too much.

---

37. Names have been changed to protect the innocent. And the guilty.
38. Not that there's anything wrong with boy bands. For instance, I rather enjoy the Beatles.

184

**Awkward Moment #5: Your date wants to date your friend.** This is awkward because, in sales, this is usually a case of your customer, the person you need to cultivate a relationship with, gravitating to the technical person or manager you brought with you. You are now the extra wheel . . . and the spare wheel usually ends up in the trunk.

If your date asks for your friend's number, that's awkward.

**(Not Quite) Example:** I don't have a love example for you here (thankfully), but I have experienced the awkward feeling of working for months to cultivate a relationship with a customer, only to have them kick me to the curb the minute they met one of my engineers. Awkward.

**Another (Not Quite) Example:** I once had a customer follow my sales engineer to the restroom and ask for "the truth"—as opposed to what they thought I had been feeding them. (Hello, LOVE LADDER!)

## Suck Less at Selling:

- Don't expect your colleagues to do your work. Invest time and energy in building credibility through strong diagnosis and discovery.

- Make sure you've got a strong business reason for the meeting. "Getting to know each other" leaves you vulnerable to awkward moments.

- Take care to get the right people together. Personal chemistry matters as much as matching job titles.

- Spend enough time planning your roles—how you'll complement each other as co-sellers and avoid the awkward moments you can.

- If it's your first double date, don't make it a cross-country road trip.

- Before you involve others, make sure your relationship is robust enough to survive those inevitable awkward moments.

# *Meeting the Parents*

In almost every complex or high-value sale, there's quite an emphasis on "meeting with the decision maker." Even the folks trying to sell you a timeshare won't meet with you unless "both decision makers are present." If they knew the real decision-making structure in my house, though, they would just ask for Donna.

And I get it. The most efficient route to a decision is to speak with the person making that decision. But is it always necessary? Raise your hand if you've done major deals where you never talked to the person that signed the purchase order. (Hands are going up.) Or where the check had a different signature than the person you sold to. (Lots of hands up.) Sometimes it's not even a good idea to go there. Talking to the boss could take you sideways or derail your sale.

## Why It's Hard to Get There

**Control.** Many customers want to maintain control of the buying relationship so they can meet their own needs and advance their own agenda. Bringing you into the executive suite could derail their agenda.

**Risk.** Letting you in to see the boss is risky. The boss has most likely paid your customer to keep pesky vendors away from them. The last thing they need is you storming in there and doing your sales thing all over their boss. Plus, the risk of your contradicting or undermining their agenda threatens their control.

If they're worried about your hitting on their mom or dad, you're less likely to get invited home for dinner.

**Saving Face.** Many customers position themselves as the decision maker in order to get you to sell to them and give them what they need early in the relationship. This boxes them into a situation where taking you to their boss is sort of like admitting they overstated their power.[39]

If he's spent a bunch of time showing you he's his "own man," but taking you home to dinner would reveal him to be a momma's boy who still lives in the basement, you may not get that invitation. (Ooh, notice the female perspective! I am versatile!)

## Why Transactionists Rarely Meet the Parents

Again, transactionists are short-form/single-sale sellers who sell and excel in a transactional environment.

**Reason #1: Transactionists don't care.** Driving a lower-level commitment often doesn't require more than a line-level decision.

---

39. Sellers often bring this on themselves by prematurely qualifying for decision authority. (See "Stay Outta My Pants!")

If you're not looking for marriage, you probably don't care if you meet the parents. In fact, you would probably prefer not to.

**Reason #2: Transactionists have tenuous staying power.** They're only as good as their last transaction, and they're perpetually vulnerable to other transactionists.

If you are the flavor of the month, why would they bring you home to meet the parents?

**Reason #3: Transactionists are after the transaction.** They're not meeting the parents to develop a relationship; they're trying to ensure future transactions. That is absolutely seller-centric.

If the only reason you want to meet the parents is so they will pressure someone to go out with you, you're not meeting the parents.

**Reason #4: Executive access increases switching costs for buyers.** Changing suppliers may force buyers to answer to executives. They can avoid this by denying access in the first place. That way, buyers maintain maximum control over the choice to change and increase their negotiating leverage.

If you're the flavor of the month, your date doesn't need the parents asking about you next month.

**Moral:** Smart transactionists are okay with this. They don't need to meet the executives, and they're not pressuring their dates to take them home to meet Mom and Dad. After all, they're only dating. They're not talking about moving in, and they don't want to change your life.

## How to Get There—Advice for Relationists

Hold on to your armrest. Some of this advice is counterintuitive . . . until you look at it through the Lens of Love, of course.

**Don't ask for permission.** Even when your ask meets the five tests of a legitimate ask, you risk coming off as seller-centric and pushy. Why? Because of the millions of salespeople who have gone before you and live around you. Asking your "Can I meet your boss?" question is a classic case of TRS (Typical Rep Syndrome).

Try these out at home: "Hey, why don't you bring your parents with you to our next date?" Or "How about introducing me to your parents?" Let me know how it goes.

**Earn the invitation instead.** When you're invited, you know you've earned the seat at the table and that you've taken it to the next level with your customer.

Being asked to join a family dinner is a much more authentic sign of commitment than if your date grudgingly gives in to your persistent begging.

**Perform your way there.** The most overlooked way of getting invited to meet with higher levels is to make your customer so happy and add so much value that they're excited to introduce you. Hint: That usually involves *not* behaving like a typical salesperson, particularly the pushy part.

You know when you get invited to meet the parents? It's when your date believes said parents will enjoy talking with you. (It's not about your enjoyment.)

**Help your customer make their internal sale.** Once your customer is convinced you're able to help them meet their own needs and advance their own agenda, access happens. The best case is a customer saying, "I need your help convincing my bosses to make the right decision."

If your presence at dinner will help your date get what they want, you're in. If not, good luck. Donna didn't invite me home to meet her parents until she was looking for their evaluation and/or approval.

**Add value to executive lives.** To be successful, you need to be able to carry a dialogue at the next level. You need to be able to discuss, focus on, and serve the needs of the executive buyer. It's what you do when you get there that gets you invited back.

If you're meeting the parents, you may want to understand and bone up on what's important to them. You know, things parents like to talk about.[40]

True story about blowing it: When I was dating my first and current spouse, Donna, she invited me to go to the Iowa State Fair with her parents. Hint that I should have taken the invite seriously: Her parents are in the Iowa 4-H Hall of Fame. Really. In other words, the fair is a big deal.

So what did I do? I showed up in my ripped jeans and backward baseball hat—you know, stuff I felt comfortable in; made wisecracks about the cows; generally violated every principle just discussed. The fact that I ultimately managed to "make the sale" happened despite what came to be known as the State Fair Debacle, not because of it. In fact, I still get grief over that incident a full twenty years later.

**Moral:** As in love, relationists in sales ultimately have their own needs met by focusing on others' needs first. This is true whether we're talking about the C-Suite or the P-Suite.

## Suck Less at Selling:

- Earn the invitation. It beats the heck out of asking for one.

- Sell in a customer-centered way and reduce the perceived risk of your meeting their boss.

- Arm yourself for the appropriate level of conversation.

- Wear nice pants.

---

40. Potential topics: your steady job, monogamy, abstinence.

# *Is It Time Yet?*

## Going for the Close

I'm gonna keep this part simple, because closing should be simple. Just like the laws of nature or the laws of physics, the laws of closing are immutable (until future discoveries render them meaningless and/or obsolete). The simplicity of the close is directly related to success. The simpler it is, the more likely you are to win.

Closing complexity is inversely related to success. (For you mathematical types, success = 1/complexity.) The more complicated you make it; the more likely you are headed for tragedy (see "Closing-Time Tragedy").

$$\text{Success} = \frac{1}{\text{Complexity}}$$

What do I mean by simplicity?
Just proposing smart next steps.
What do I mean by complexity?
Anything that isn't just proposing smart next steps.

## Satisfy the Why, and the How Is Easy

Too many words have been written on closing techniques, by "gurus" who live in a mythical world of magical lines and guaranteed tricks. In reality, closing techniques are like snowflakes: they're all unique. Beware the charlatan that tries to sell you their way to close.

If you've ever tried to use a pickup line that someone told you was foolproof, you are probably the proof that it's not.

My advice: Satisfy the conditions that lead to closing, and closing techniques themselves are secondary. The answer to "Is it time yet?" depends on certain factors.

Is your timing right? It is when these happen:

**You both see the match**. In other words, the customer must see the value *before* you close. You're not going to convince them by the act of closing. Save closing arguments for the jury.

Before you spend all that money on a ring, perhaps you should be sure you're gonna get a "yes."

**You're talking to the right person**. If they see the match but can't pull the trigger, you are closing the wrong person. Ask decision makers for decisions; ask advocates for advocacy.

If you want to marry someone, don't propose to their younger sibling.

**There's nothing superseding the decision.** You're not closing in a vacuum. If the customer is dealing with more urgent issues, you may get rejected/postponed even though the other conditions are met.

If they need to finish school first, be sensitive to that. Especially if it's high school.

So think of "the right time" as a combination of factors that make it the right time.

## Suck Less at Selling:

- Keep closing simple.

- Propose smart next steps.

## Q and A

Q: But Dan, most of the people I know proposed to their beloved in a special way. Why, you yourself proposed to Donna on an airplane where everybody had been secretly given a sign to wave that read, "Say Yes!" How does this jibe with your law of simplicity?

A: You got me. I wrote this question. And I did propose to Donna in exactly that way. But I'll share a dirty little secret the engagement ring people probably don't want publicized: the ring, the romantic dinner, the plane full of sign-waving people, the unicorns—they're all unnecessary. Yes is yes with or without the romantic dinner, and no is no, unicorns or no unicorns. In fact, my friend *the Julio* (not his real name) was proposed to in a car. In a shopping mall parking lot. On a weeknight. No dinner. No ring. No unicorns. He said yes, and they're still happily married as of this writing. The point is, in either case, fancy or simple, the closing conditions were met. It was time.

Q: But Dan, what about the time-honored practice of asking parental permission to marry someone? Didn't you your-self ask for Donna's hand in marriage before you actually proposed?

A: Okay, so I wrote this question too. And I did do exactly that—while watching steers parade around the show ring at the Iowa Beef Expo (her father's natural habitat). But I'll be frank: in most cases, this step is a "nice to have," not a neces-sary condition of marriage. I was confirming advocacy, not closing the deal. Plus, I was in early, infatuation love—his reaction wasn't necessarily going to deter me.

# *The Selling Never Stops*

I've talked a lot in this book about things like listening, under-standing the need before you offer solutions, the power of customers saying/seeing it for themselves, and so on. Now I'm here to tell you those things are *always* true. They're true no matter how long you've known someone, how well you know someone, or how effective or valuable your solutions are.

What do I mean by this? Perhaps a little story would help. This time, we'll lead with the Lens of Love and translate back to business . . .

Several weeks ago, Donna came home from a meeting. I was in the office working when she came in and dropped wearily into a chair. Here's how the conversation went:

> **Me (still staring at computer screen):** Hey, honey, how was your meeting?
>
> **Donna:** Not great. [Name withheld] threw me under the bus. Totally blamed me for a problem they helped create.
>
> **Me:** Uh-huh.
>
> **Donna:** That really ticks me off. You know what I'm saying?

**Me (finally looking up from computer):** You've just got to call that stuff out in the meeting. Give it right back to 'em. Otherwise, they'll just do it again next time.

**Donna:** But we already have enough division on the team. I don't think another argument about who's at fault is good for the group.

**Me:** You've just got to be diplomatic in how you do it. For instance, I would use a question like . . .

**Donna (slightly irritated):** I'm sure you would, but it's still defensive behavior from me, and I don't want to be perceived that way.

**Me (überconfidently):** Hey, I've dealt with this a hundred times. You've got to nip that stuff in the bud, or it's going to come up again and again, and it's going to hurt your standing with the group more than fighting back now would.

**Donna (definitely irritated):** You just don't understand.

Ouch. Not my brightest shining moment as a spouse. Let's review:

- I have known Donna for a long time.

- I know all about Donna and that she's more than capable of standing up for herself in a meeting.

- My advice was technically correct.

The business parallel to this story happens all the time too. Your longtime customer comes to you with a need or an issue. You see the solution immediately based on your knowledge of the customer, so you offer it. Strangely (to you), your beautiful solution is resisted or rejected.

The problem, in both cases, is that we fall into certain *assumptive traps* that diminish our effectiveness and potentially damage the relationship. What are these traps?

**Assumptive Trap #1: Assuming the need.** Just because you see the need doesn't mean the customer sees the need. The trap happens when the customer's perception of their needs evolves or changes, and ours doesn't. Needs are dynamic, not static. Thus, needs assessment and validating the customer's needs should never stop.

Lovers, don't confuse "I need to tell you something" with "I need your advice on what to do about it."

**Assumptive Trap #2: Assuming we've earned the right to prescribe solutions.** Just because you know the customer super well doesn't mean you've earned the right to prescribe solutions. You know what earns you the right? Good diagnosis. If you've had the same physician for twenty years, do they stop examining you and just prescribe medication? Even if you wish it were so (depending on the medication), that would be malpractice.

Prescription without diagnosis is malpractice in love as well as medicine.

**Assumptive Trap #3: Assuming the customer wants our advice.** Just because the customer is coming to you with an issue doesn't mean the customer is interested in your solutions. For example, a customer with intimate knowledge of your company and process may come to you with a complaint or issue they know you can't resolve. It's interesting to see how often they just want to have their experience heard and acknowledged. Of course, sometimes they want resolution and ideas. The point is, being able to tell the difference is key to avoiding giving unsolicited advice.

I continue to be surprised by how often Donna just wants me to validate her feelings and ideas. My favorite question: "Donna, are you looking for my advice here?" I continue to be shocked by how often the answer is "no."

## The Sometimes Avoidable Tragedy: "We've Grown Apart"

In both business and love, growing apart is a serious, pervasive issue. Sometimes it's unavoidable; sometimes it's not.

**Unavoidable**

- The customer no longer needs what you have to offer.

- A competitor can meet your customer's needs better than you can.

- Your company's priorities or capabilities change.

**Avoidable**

- You stop listening to and engaging the customer.

- You take your eye off the need.

- You fail to anticipate the customer's changing priorities.

This is a short chapter because the key is simple: EFFORT. Continuing to put your best effort into the relationship ensures you're avoiding the troubles that come from inattentiveness. At the same time, you're much more likely to be clear on where you're just not right for each other anymore. But the key is continuous, diligent effort over time.

So, your challenge as a seller is this: avoid the avoidable, accept the unavoidable, and know which is which. Sort of the sales version of the Serenity Prayer:

*Give me the serenity to accept the deals I cannot close, the courage to close the deals I can, and the wisdom to know the difference.*

## Suck Less at Selling:

- Use the skills that got you there: good diagnosis and needs assessment. They're the same skills that will keep you there.

- Treat needs as dynamic, not static. Constantly reexamine what your customers are really looking for and what they value.

- Assume the need for your listening. Confirm the need for your solutions and advice.

- Use the principles of serenity, both in selling and in life.

- Don't stop your believing. You must hold on to that feeling. It's a . . . Journey.[41]

- Try.

---

41. Yeah, I just did that. From my '80s pop-culture puns there is no . . . *Escape*.

# PART
# FIVE

*Getting Dumped, Breaking Up,
and Other Tragedies*

# Is She Really Going Out with Him?

*Our envy always lasts longer than the happiness
of those we envy.*

—François de La Rochefoucauld

*Jealousy is love in competition.*

—Toba Beta

Want a strong visual reference for this chapter? Go to YouTube and search for Joe Jackson's song "Is She Really Going Out with Him?" If you're not that ambitious, imagine this dude doing a spit take as he sees his prospective honey walking down the street with someone else. Whether you've experienced this in love or selling (or both, as I have), it's not a good feeling. Let's examine the feeling using the ever-popular stages of grief model.

Note to sensitive readers: As always, I will be speaking from the perspective of the adolescent male, which (a) all males can relate to, and (b) might be useful to my female readers as a means of understanding the male psyche.

Note to other sensitive readers: For this discussion, I will also be referring to the object of one's affection as *she*, because (a) that's my frame of reference, and (b) all my favorite songs are written that way.

## Stage 1: Denial

Sales version: "They must have an opt-out clause in the contract. I can still close it."

Love version: "She's just using him for his money (or car, fake ID, etc.). I still have a chance."

## Stage 2: Grief

Sales version: "Aaaaaaaaaaah!" followed by forecast adjustments/five "Why?" analysis/management second-guessing/blaming your price/putting your résumé together.

Love version: "Aaaaaaaaaah!" followed by browbeating/second-guessing/monopolizing BFF conversations with your loneliness/resulting apathy/questionable will to live.

## Stage 3: Anger

Sales version: You complain to your boss about how shady the competition is. You swear that you were never gonna win anyway, because it was all about price, and this deal proves it. You're mad because your forecast is ruined, and you won't make quota/President's Club.

Love version: You complain to your friends about what a loser the winner is. You swear that you didn't want her anyway, that she isn't good enough for you, and this proves it. You're mad because this ruins your plans for homecoming/prom/life.

## Stage 4: Acceptance

Actually, I wouldn't know about this one. I've never made it this far. I hear there's even another stage after this one.

Anyway, the first three stages are the important ones for salespeople, for three reasons.

1. **Denial kills**—and kills your wallet. Those of us who have burned a lunch/round of golf/wrist corsage/ proposal on a nonprospect will relate. (Again, that may have been just me.)

2. **Grief is useful** because it teaches you things. It's just not enjoyable.

3. **Anger is a reaction**, and reactions are dangerous things in both love and selling. In fact, some of the biggest competitive blunders I've seen in professional selling have been the result of rash action at this stage.

## What Would You Do?

In my sales training workshops, I often confront sellers with this scenario:

You've been courting a prospect for months. You've put your best foot forward. You've spent time, money, and organizational resources. The prospect has seen samples and received references and case studies. You've met with all the right people. You've put a top-flight proposal out there, complete with your very best pricing.

Then you get the dreaded "Dear Seller" voice mail: "Thanks for everything, but we've decided to go in another direction. Your solution is great, but we just felt that your competitor's offering is a better fit for our needs at this time. You've really been great, and I enjoyed working with you. We'll let you know if our needs change down the road."[42]

Let's look at the most common responses I get from sellers. To examine potential effectiveness, we'll use the ever-handy Lens of Love to see how that's really working for you. (Admit it—you've done some of these.)

## Typical Responses:

- Call the prospect back right away and try to get them on the phone. Failing that, show up at their office/home.

- Try to find out what the prospect means by "decided." Has a purchase order been cut?

- Find out what happened. What about the samples/references/proposal they loved?

- Try to find out what you missed. Was it something in particular they didn't see?

---

42. More realistic version: the customer goes silent, and you learn later that they bought from someone else.

- Ask if you can have another opportunity to show the value of your solution.

- Call your internal advocate and see if they can help reverse the decision.

- Attempt to enlighten the prospect as to the potential shortfalls of buying from your competitor. Encourage prospect to check references thoroughly.

- Attempt to reopen the deal by improving the terms of your offer.

- As a last-ditch effort, call above your contact in the hopes of getting the decision reversed at executive levels.

- Have your boss call the prospect.

Each of these responses, in love, could potentially be classified as "creepy."

Are you getting my drift? Viewed through the Lens of Love, these typical responses (which many of your managers are unfortunately asking you for) start to look fairly ridiculous. Which they are. Unless you are going for the desperate vibe, seriously reconsider the use of any of these strategies.

So what's left?

## Take the High Road

What's left are two less-typical responses, both of which represent the high road in selling:

**Atypical Response #1:** Don't call them back.

**Why This Could Work:** Let's face it—the prospect is probably not looking forward to a call from you. Spare them the agony and discomfort, and you may improve your long-term chances.

Anything you can do to avoid seeming desperate helps your personal brand. Even if you're, you know, desperate.

**Atypical Response #2:** Write them a thank-you note—a gracious thank-you that doesn't include any of the typical responses we just went through.

**Why This Could Work:** First, it's not typical and somewhat disarming to a prospect who's bracing for the typical set of responses from you, the jilted seller. Second, it's durable. Most people who receive thank-you notes (and there are few) read them more than once and even keep them for a while.

Don't you want their last taste of you to be a sweet one?

**Atypical Response #3:** Offer to be there when they need you. Imply, but don't state, the possibility that things might not work out with their first choice.

**Why This Could Work:** Even if you're correct about the competition's faults, you're the least likely to be believed. You're a sore loser! Instead, be the gracious loser and wait for time and experience to prove you right.

Leave the door open. You never know who will come walking back through it.

**Atypical Response #4:** Seek to understand why you lost *without* arguing.

**Why This Could Work:** The first part is typical (and typically required by your boss); the second part is not. Suppressing the urge to change their mind (you probably won't) will be a pleasant surprise and increase your chances of getting back together someday.

You know why they make up reasons? It's because you can't handle the truth.[43]

**Atypical Response #5:** Congratulate them and wish them well.

**Why This Could Work:** Gracious losers are more likely to get a second shot.

The precious dove of your affection will return to the welcoming branches of the gracious tree and avoid the prickly grasping of the scorned shrub.

## Competing When You're Not Winning: Strategies for Love and Selling

**Prevention Strategy:** Use leading indicators to see where you're getting outsold and whether customers are really buying what you're selling. It's about whether they need you enough and whether they're doing anything to move in your direction. (For

---

43. It's not you; it's me. I just need some space. You know, to find myself . . .

those of us who must communicate in business speak: value and commitment.)

Business example: Use the customer's willingness to take first steps as an indicator of their willingness to take the final step.

Be clear about the level of reciprocal commitment you're getting. If your potential mate has never asked *you* out, you may want to hold up on that marriage proposal.

**Effectiveness Strategy:** Get better at what you do so you win more and lose less (and thus have less grief to deal with).

Business examples: Produce better products. Market more effectively. Sell better. Offer value pricing. Have meetings that are about more than your selling them stuff.

Lose a little weight. Turn off the PlayStation. Learn some manners. Offer dinner for a change. Heading over to Inspiration Point for a make-out session is not necessarily a date.

**Abundance Strategy:** Prospect "more than enough" and you will care less about the loss of any individual prospect. Useful in sales, where you're paid to be polygamous. Useful also in love unless you believe, like the swan, that there is only one true soul mate for you. Raise your hand if someone has told you, "There are other fish in the sea." Sounds right to me, salespeople. (Swans, that's a tough one.)

Business example: Have so many prospects that the loss of any one prospect will not break you.

If more than one person would go to the dance with you, you don't have to beg any single person.

**Dignity Strategy:** Focus on what's best for your *long-term* relationship, and that means losing with dignity and class. Refuse to speak badly about either party. Avoid desperate offers. No whining. Crying won't help. Sometimes your prospective mate needs to have a bad experience with someone else to appreciate your value. She won't if you're stalking her in the meantime.

Business example: Have some dignity. Pull yourself together. Don't be desperate.

Ditto on the dignity part. Desperation is unbecoming.

## Suck Less at Selling:

- Have enough deals in your pipeline to survive the loss of any single deal.

- Sell to who's buying, and minimize your investment elsewhere.

- Avoid the cringe-worthy behaviors of the typical scorned seller. They're unbecoming.

- Lose with dignity and thus set the stage for future wins.

# Closing-Time Tragedies

Oh, yes! We're talkin' 'bout closing! Every seller's favorite part! Money time!

Well, yes and no. Yes, if we're talking about a transactional sale, the sales equivalent of the one-night stand. Not necessarily, if we're talking about the relationship sale, the sales equivalent of love and marriage. Let's review those distinctions:

| TRANSACTIONAL SALE (ONE-NIGHT STAND) CLOSING | RELATIONSHIP SALE (LOVE AND MARRIAGE) CLOSING |
|---|---|
| • customary | • not customary |
| • expected–there is no "too early" | • there is definitely a "too early" |
| • fast | • patient and disciplined |
| • numbers game–you've got to close enough to be successful | • effectiveness game–you've got to earn the privilege of closing |
| • no meeting the parents | • meeting parents could be required |
| • one close in one call | • multiple incremental closes over multiple calls |
| • sellers attempt to close customers | • customers close themselves |

The point: There's a distinct difference between the all-or-nothing closing that happens in a transactional sale and the incremental closing that occurs in a relationship sale.

I've watched a lot of salespeople close, or attempt to close, and the results are often, well, tragic. And by tragic, I mean this:

- disastrous

- sad

- painful

- calamitous

- pathetic

Let's look at some of the most common *closing tragedies* in selling. Just like a Greek tragedy, many closing attempts are often dramatic events that involve suffering by both seller and customer and provoke an accompanying feeling of either catharsis or pleasure in the witness. Doesn't that sound fun?

## The Tragedy of Misunderstanding

Now, I'm no student of ancient literature, but I do distinctly remember both reading and seeing a performance of Shakespeare's *Romeo and Juliet* in sixth grade. And as I recall, a major contributing factor to that tragedy was a series of misunderstandings about what was really happening.

In closing (and, of course, in love!), there are two major types of misunderstandings that lead to tragedy.

## Misunderstanding #1: Treating a relationship sale like a transactional sale

|  | BUSINESS EXAMPLE | LENS OF LOVE |
|---|---|---|
| *Causes* | Quotas and deadlines | Hormones and alcohol |
| *Results In* | Premature closing, rejection | Inappropriate closing, face slapping |
| *Tragic Because* | You just blew it with your best prospect | You just blew it with your potential soul mate |

Of course, it works the other way too.

## Misunderstanding #2: Treating a transactional sale like a relationship sale

|  | BUSINESS EXAMPLE | LENS OF LOVE |
|---|---|---|
| *Causes* | Not picking up on buying signals; fear of closing | Not picking up on buying signals; timidity and fear |
| *Results In* | Buyer chooses your competitor | They go home with that jerk |
| *Tragic Because* | You could have made a sale right now | You could be getting lucky right now |

The point: Pay more attention to the customer, understand what the game is, and close (or don't close) accordingly.

## The Tragedy of Closing Techniques

No matter what kind of sale you're in, most of the classic closing techniques I've witnessed are classic only in their tragicness (Tragicity? Tragicesqueness?). Let's examine some classics.

### Tragic Closing Technique #1: The If-Then Question

Business example: "If I lowered the price to X, would you buy today?"

"If I said you had a beautiful body, would you hold it against me?"

My advice: Ick. Don't ask those. Stop using the if-then question right now.

### Tragic Closing Technique #2: Dangling a Benefit

Business example: "If you sign today, you can start receiving the benefits right away."

"If you go home with me, you could be gettin' some of this." (points to self)

My advice: Again, ick. Benefits are in the eye of the customer, not yours. Stop that.

### Tragic Closing Technique #3: The Expiring Offer

Business example: "This price will go up tomorrow. This is your only chance to get this price."

"I'm leaving for war in the morning. This is your only chance to get with me."

My advice: *Iiiiiiiiick*. You and I both know that's probably a lie, anyway. Don't!

## Tragic Closing Technique #4: Doing Things for the Customer So You Can Guilt Them into Buying

Business example: Wining and dining the customer and then bringing it up if they hesitate to buy.

"Hey, what about all those drinks I bought you?"

My advice: Wow. Just wow. Please desist.

## Tragic Closing Technique #5: Any Closing "Line" That Customers Have Heard Before

Business example: Don't trust sales books that offer you "secrets to closing the sale" or "ten questions that close the sale." If it's not coming from you, it's just a line, and it's not authentic.

Beware the pop-up ad or *Cosmopolitan* article that promises "secrets." News flash—it's not a secret!

My advice: Be yourself. Be authentic. Be straightforward. And see my next book, *Twenty-One Guaranteed Secret Closing Tricks*, for more surefire techniques.[44]

---

44. I am joking.

## The Tragedy of "Too Soon"

Simply put, this is the tragedy of the premature close. The customer is not ready or willing, but you're going for it anyway. While this is much more common in the relationship sale, it happens in the transactional sale too. Even in the retail setting, an early trial close is a turnoff and sends many running for the exit.

This tragedy occurs for three reasons:

**Reason #1:** You're too focused on your own agenda/quota/time line.

You're lonely, horny, and/or drunk.

**Reason #2:** You misread the customer's polite curiosity as a buying signal.

They didn't reject you outright, so they must be into you.

**Reason #3:** You assume that letting you sell to them means they want to buy from you.

They let you buy them a drink! Of course they're into you!

The premature close has three possible outcomes, two of which are undesirable. Let's start with the happy one:

**Outcome #1: You get lucky.** The customer wants to buy for the right reasons. Congratulations!

**Outcome #2: Rejection.** You are rebuffed, perhaps for good. Ouch. (Note: Some of you are thinking, "Dan, a *no* is just the first step toward a *yes*." I encourage you to examine that thinking through the Lens of Love.)

**Outcome #3: You are successful but for the wrong reasons.**

For more on this last one, let's look at our third and final tragedy . . .

## The Tragedy of Regret, a.k.a. "What Have I Done?"

This is an underrated tragedy, mainly because its effects are often not felt until later or much later. Let's look at some versions of this tragedy. Grab your Lens of Love and come along!

**Version #1—Immediate Regret:** You make a sale to someone you wish you hadn't. In your rush to close, you lower your standards and land a deal you shouldn't have. In selling, you (or your company) may attempt to renege on or renegotiate the deal (although you may be trapped by this point).

You wake up the morning after "closing the deal." You take a look at who you landed with and immediately attempt to flee. (Could include the desire to chew your arm off to escape.)

**Version #2—Eventual Regret:** You make a sale for the wrong reasons (for example, price) and in time come to regret the decision because of its long-term impact. In selling, you spend inordinate amounts of time dealing with issues, things end badly, and you get flamed on Internet discussion boards.

You end up in a bad relationship, you fight all the time, and eventually break up/divorce. You get flamed on social media.

**Summary:** That's what happens when you rush to the close, do anything to close, and ignore potential danger signals. Even "getting lucky" today involves risk.

So what do you do about all this?

## Suck Less at Selling:

- Know what type of relationship your customer is after and sell accordingly.

- Avoid assumptions that lead to inappropriate or premature closing.

- Don't mistake politeness or curiosity for commitment.

- Have enough pipeline/prospects that you don't feel pressure to close any single prospect.

- Pause to make sure you're closing the right customer for the right reasons.

- Ditch the cheesy, sleazy closing techniques.

# Getting Paid or Getting Played?

When I conduct sales training workshops, I often ask people, "What are sellers paid to do?"

"Close!" they shout, almost in unison. When I ask what that means, they shout, "Close the deal!"

"But what does *that* mean? Particularly in a complex sale or a sale that takes more than one close? Does that mean that if you fail to close, you've failed the sales call?" I ask with eyebrow raised to demonstrate my skepticism.

"No, trainer boy," they say gently as if to humor me, "you can have a successful call that doesn't close if you move it to the next step."

"And what are some examples of next steps?" I ask.

They patiently lay out a laundry list. "Scheduling the next meeting." "Sending a proposal." "Making a benchmark." "Providing budget figures and references."

Well, my skeptical eyebrow is still up. Why? Before I answer that, let's take a look at what sellers are paid to do.

## Sellers Are Paid to Get Commitments over Time

I submit that what you're really paid to do, and the *only* thing you're paid to do, is get commitment. Everything else is just a means to this end. Getting the customer to sign a deal or place an order, of course, is the most clear-cut and obvious example of getting commitment. But you're also paid to get the commitments along the way that lead to the ultimate commitment of a buy. Notice that I just said "the ultimate commitment of a *buy*," not "a sale."

## Sellers Are Working against Time

If companies were not trying to reduce the time it takes customers to go from "unaware you exist" to "happy, loyal customer," there would be no salespeople. There would just be marketing and order entry. (And indeed, this is the case in the online retail world.)

If your company has hired you to *sell*, though, you're probably being evaluated against time.

- You have a quota—how much you're supposed to sell in a given time.

- You have deadlines—your quota must be achieved (or not) by a certain date.

- You have sales cycle length—many sales leaders evaluate your success based on how long it takes you to get a deal done. "Faster" sellers are glorified; "slower" sellers get put on a performance improvement plan until they get "faster."

## Sellers Are Not Paid to Sell

Yeah, you heard me. I said you're not paid to sell. Let's break it down:

- Sellers are paid when customers make commitments.

- Selling is something sellers do, not what customers do.

- Therefore, while you're often *required* to utilize sales behaviors, you're not *paid* to do so.

- In other words, *you're paid to help customers buy.*

You know how I know it's true? Some of the very best, the very most productive, and the most highly *paid* salespeople I know use some sales behaviors *less often* than their colleagues:

- I once conducted a study with a major tech manufacturer that revealed that the top 20 percent of sales reps (by revenue) sent 34 percent fewer proposals than their average peers. In other words, there was not a correlation between more sales behaviors and more sales (or more pay for the salesperson).

- In many telephone-based sales that involve more than one phone call, there is not a correlation between dials and sales. Top salespeople often aren't making the most calls. In other words, there is often not a correlation between more sales behaviors and more sales.

In short, *selling* as we've always defined it (open, qualify, assess needs, present solutions, negotiate, close) is *not* what you're paid to do. It's merely a means to an end. And misapplication of the means, as we're about to find out, leads to undesirable ends. Embarrassing, regret-laden, stalkeresque ends . . .

## An All-Too-Familiar Sales Scenario

As we walk through a typical sales process, I want you to think about this diagram:

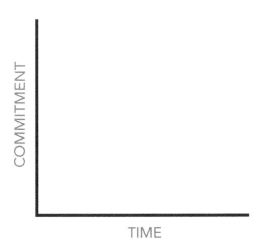

THE SALES PROCESS

Feel free to draw the progression of seller and buyer.[45] In the following scenario, who is moving up the commitment scale (Y axis) at what time (X axis)?

(Note: Although I'm sure you've never personally done this, I will say *you*. When I say *you*, it's for illustration purposes. I'm not accusing you of sucking at selling.)

---

45. Or mentally draw, ebook readers!

### Step #1: Contact

You: "Hello, Prospect? How you doin'? I'm with so-and-so company, and I'd love to talk with you about our solutions and how they might fit your needs. Can I come by and introduce myself?"

Prospect: "Sure. Come on in. Next Tuesday at 9:00 a.m."

### Step #2: Meeting (Tuesday, 9:00 a.m.)

You: Rapport-building ("Nice fish. Where'd you catch it?"). Qualifying ("Are you the person who makes the decision? How does that work?"). Needs assessment ("Would you like to improve how you're doing it today?"). Demonstrating the solution ("Based on what you told me, our solution could really help, and here's how"). Closing ("How about another meeting with your boss/your team?").

Prospect: "Why don't you send me some more information on that solution? I'm interested. Follow up with me in a week."

### Step #3: Follow-Up (One Week Later)

You: "How did you like that information I sent you? How about a meeting with your boss/team?"

Prospect: "Haven't read your info, but I'm interested. Sure. Let's meet. Bring your technical expert. Tuesday at 9:00 a.m."

### Step #4: Technical Meeting (One Week Later, Tuesday, 9:00 a.m.)

You (and your technical expert): Answer the prospect's questions. Qualify further. Elaborate on your solutions. Ask for next steps.

Prospect: "I'm very interested. Why don't you make me a proposal, and I'll need your very best price. Oh, you want to present it? Sure. Tuesday at 9:00 a.m."

## Step #5: Proposal Presentation (Two Weeks Later, Tuesday, 9:00 a.m.)

You (and your boss): Present the proposal. Field questions about price, implementation, etc. Ask for next steps.

Prospect: "We're very interested, but we need to think about this. Follow up in a week. How about Tuesday at 9:00 a.m.?"

## Step #6: Follow-Up (One Week Later, Tuesday, 9:00 a.m.)

You: "What do you think? Are you ready to go ahead with it?"

Prospect: "Perhaps—we're super interested. Can you send me some references? Get back with me in a week. Tuesday at 9:00 a.m. works."

## Step #7: References Follow-Up (Tuesday, 9:00 a.m.)

You (leaving a voice mail): "Did you have a chance to talk to those references? What's our status?"

## Step #8: Follow-Up (Last Tuesday of the Month, 9:00 a.m.)

You (voice mail): "Umm, just checking in to see how things are going. Let me know."

## Steps #9–#12: Follow-Up (Last Tuesday of the Quarter, 9:00 a.m.)

You (voice mail): "Listen, it's coming up on the end of the quarter, and I'm just wondering where we stand."

## Step #13: Contact!

You: "Hey, I finally got a hold of you! So, are you ready to go ahead with it?"

Prospect: "Not quite yet. We've had some other things come up, but we're absolutely still interested. Why don't you give me a call in about 90 days, and we should be ready to go by then."

When I describe this little scenario, three things usually happen:

- Salespeople shift around in their chairs and giggle uncomfortably.

- Salespeople wince as they remember this.

- Salespeople ask me, "Have you been on sales calls with us?"[46]

The truth is, this is typical of a lot of sales processes. Certainly, the seller is engaged in a sales process, but how's the buying process going?

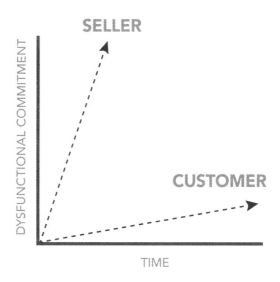

To illustrate in terms we can all understand . . . look out, here it comes!

46. The answer? "Probably."

If this scenario described you and a boy/girl you liked, would you say you are dating?

Spoiler alert: You are *not dating*! You are *stalking*! You are only dating in your mind! You have a tux and a wrist corsage but no prom date!

You know what's amazing to me? I've witnessed this process play out literally hundreds of times, and when I ask sellers how they'd forecast their chances, I get some form of "I'm closing them next quarter."

"How so?" I ask innocently.

The seller (not you, of course) responds, "Well, they're definitely qualified. I'm talking to the decision maker. They obviously need our solution. They've seen our demo and talked to my tech, they've got our proposal and pricing, and they're super interested. I'll get 'em next quarter."

Meanwhile, the "prospect" has politely endured your sales calls, enjoyed your free consulting, and received some useful benchmarking information they can use to keep their current vendor honest. Again, I ask, are you really dating? *You are not.*

So what happened? How did this turn from selling into stalking?

## Four Reasons Sellers Get Played, Not Paid

### Reason #1: Failure to Differentiate Interest from Commitment

It's easy to get lulled into a false sense of optimism by a prospect who seems to be interested in buying from you. In fact, experienced customers will use that fact to their advantage. If they can squeeze a whole lotta free consulting out of you by simply professing their interest, why not? Their job is to get value from their time with you, and free consulting in exchange for interest is a good deal for them. The problem occurs when that interest is not accompanied by action on the part of the customer. If professions of interest aren't backed up by customer action, you may be selling, but the customer isn't buying.

If your prospective mate says they're excited about your date, but when you show up Friday night, they're like, "Oh, yeah . . . I'm actually flossing my cat right now. Can we postpone by a week? Because I'm really excited about our date." You may be getting played, not paid.

### *Reason #2: Gauging Success by Seller Next Steps, Not Customer Next Steps*

Another reason sellers get fooled is that they use their own next steps as the measurement of success, when success is really about what the customer does because of your sales effort. In other words, your sales *inputs* are necessary and swell, but it's the *outcomes*—what customers do because of your inputs—that really determine your success. After all, you're paid on the commitments customers make, not on the commitments you make. If you're putting in a lot of sales effort but not seeing the outcomes in terms of customer commitment, you may be selling, but the customer isn't buying.

If your prospective mate allows you to buy them fancy dinners but never kisses you good night, you may be getting played, not paid. (Note that I am not suggesting they're *required* to kiss you back; just wondering if they *want* to.)

### Reason #3: Failing to Get Reciprocal Commitment

Remember earlier when we discussed what sellers are paid to do? (Okay, it wasn't really a discussion . . . unless you were answering me. And, of course, I couldn't hear you.)

That's right. I said you are paid to *get commitment.*

When you offer to do something for the customer, and they accept, it's reasonable to ask for a reciprocal commitment. Something along the lines of "Please help me get you what you want." If it meets the customer's need, it's perfectly legitimate for you to propose it.

---

**FIVE TESTS OF A LEGITIMATE "ASK"**

Will it help the customer get what they want?

Can they do it?

Does it make logical sense?

Is now the right time?

Do they want to do it?

---

Likewise, if the customer is asking you for something, there's no better time to propose a legitimate reciprocal commitment.

Again, it's a matter of "Help me help you, so you can . . ." If it meets the five tests of a legitimate "ask," propose it.

If your prospective mate wants you to take them somewhere fancy, it's reasonable to ask them to pack accordingly.

### Reason #4: Sales Goggles

Have you ever noticed the phenomenon of how the closer it gets to the end of the month/quarter/year, the more you think you're going to close a particular deal? It's almost as if you project your impending deadlines onto the customer. And the closer the deadline, the better everyone starts to look. As the deadline nears, suspects start to look like prospects to the lonely seller. The pressures of time have the potential to produce an ironic effect: the closer you are to a deadline, the more you're likely to focus on your own needs and not the reality of what's happening with the customer. Hence, sales goggles.

Sales goggles have a number of unfortunate side effects:

- proposing commitments customers aren't ready to make

- attempting to "sweeten the deal" in an attempt to force a decision

- cheesy sales techniques like the expiring offer

- begging

- rejection and loss of face

- a deal that you shouldn't have made and will regret later

Ouch. If you're proposing commitments based on your need to make quota and not the needs of the customer, you're in danger of getting played, not paid.

You're at the club. You've met this new prospective mate, and you're totally into them. All of a sudden, the lights go up. Closing time. Cue the cheesy closing techniques. Or was that just me?

All of these unfortunate situations, of course, are preventable. Maybe not in love. That's your business. In terms of business . . .

## Suck Less at Selling:

- Understand customer milestones.

- Set goals and measure results in customer next steps, not seller next steps.

- Propose reciprocal commitment.

- Forecast according to the customer's actions, not yours.

## Q and A

**Q:** But Dan, aren't sellers paid to "make the first move"?

**A:** Of course you are. Sellers lead the dance. But if you're the only one making moves, you are dancing alone. That's not what you're paid to do, and it's also sort of awkward.

**Q:** But Dan, I can't demand my customers take on action items at the end of my calls.

**A:** You're right. Instead of demanding, simply propose customer next steps that meet the five tests of a legitimate ask. They either will or they won't.

**Q:** But Dan, I propose next steps all the time, and my customers don't do them.

**A:** Of course this happens. When it does, ask yourself these two questions:

- Did my ask meet the five tests of a legitimate ask? (If not, your fault.)

- If it did and they didn't, what have I learned about my real prospects? (You may be learning that they're not a real prospect.)

# The Curse of the Premature

Perhaps the most fundamental plague on the sales profession is the curse of the premature. In a nutshell, salespeople earn their reputations as cheesy, pushy, and aggressive when they succumb to certain, ah, urges. Let's take a closer look at three main varieties of this curse. And they are indeed curses. Then, of course, we will look at these same curses through the Lens of Love.

A Note on the Lens of Love: The Lens of Love is *not* the Lens of Sex. Although most people can't help but giggle at the very use of the word *premature*, you'll have to fill in the, ah, naughty bits yourself . . . unless they work their way into the conversation somehow.

## The Curse of Premature Elaboration

**Definition:** Premature elaboration is the unwanted early description of the seller's features and potential benefits. Also known as "showing up and throwing up."

**Cause:** Usually caused by either a lack of awareness or indifference as to whether the customer is ready to hear it.

**Why It's Bad:** Often elaborating on solutions signals the end of the process. Customers could evaluate your offering in the absence of need and either object or dismiss you. If you shoot your gun too early, you may not make it to the next round.

**Why Salespeople Don't Get It:** If you're the seller tossing solutions all over the place, it feels good. It's something you know intimately. You're good at it. It's easy to lose focus on whether the customer is digging your elaboration like you're digging your own elaboration.

**Just a Tip:** Can you hold off until the customer is truly ready for your elaboration? Can you focus on the less-comfortable work of building the heat on the needs that lead to value? Can you at least think of baseball?

(Thinking . . .)

I can't even go there.

## The Curse of the Premature Solution

**Definition:** Premature solutioning is the offer to solve a customer's problem before the customer has fully recognized the problem. Also known as *unsolicited advice*.

**Cause:** Usually caused by the seller's experience. You've seen it before. Also caused by seller-centeredness (you care more about your advice than the customer's appetite for it) or impending deadlines (you feel pressure to close).

**Why It's Bad:** Customers object to advice for two reasons: it's either bad advice, or they're not ready to hear it. In either case, you lose. The real tragedy is when you're offering excellent advice too early—you could have made the sale if only you had held out!

**Why Salespeople Don't Get It:** When you see the answer, your mind tends to stop asking the questions. And the question that rarely gets asked at that point is, "Is the customer ready to hear my opinion?"

**Just a Tip:** Can you test for receptiveness to your advice? How about a question like "Is this something you're trying to solve?" Or "Are you looking for advice or help with this?"[47]

One of the biggest disconnects in a relationship is when one party wants to be heard and the other party just wants to solve the problem. The result is insufficient listening and, at least in my house, rejection of some perfectly (I think) good advice.

## The Curse of the Premature Close

**Definition:** Premature closing is attempting to gain customer commitment in the absence of key prerequisites: right person, right time, right action, right reason. (See the sidebar "Five tests of a legitimate 'ask.'")

**Cause:** Usually caused by the seller's impatience. You're anxious to get a deal done, take the next steps, or take it to the next level. Reasons range from internal (you're just impatient) to external (your boss is impatient). Deadlines, quotas, and commissions are common contributing factors.

**Why It's Bad:** Premature closing is where you give up every gain you've made in terms of good diagnosing, solution developing,

---

47. Keep in mind the risk of asking questions you read in a sales book. Make your own chili.

and relationship building. You end up looking like the typical pushy, needy salesperson.

**Why Salespeople Don't Get It:** The noise of your own needs (or your boss's needs) drowns out everything else. The closer you get to what you *think* should be closing time, the less you tend to focus on whether it's commitment time for the customer.

**Just a Tip:** Pause. Take a moment. Consider how well the four prerequisites (person, timing, action, reason) are really lined up. Are you sure it's time to close?

> If you don't know what the answer will be, perhaps you aren't ready to propose. Don't pop for the engagement ring unless you know you've got a yes—those suckers are hard to return. Or so I hear.

## Suck Less at Selling:

- Don't take your eyes and ears off the customer's needs the minute you think you've got an opportunity.

- Ask yourself, "Is it time yet?"

- Then ask yourself, "Is it *really* time yet?"

- Just to be safe, ask yourself one more time.

# *Breaking Up Is Hard to Do*

In this chapter, I discuss a counterintuitive but critical competency of the effective seller: differentiating prospects from suspects and treating them differently—selling to prospects and cutting the suspects loose.

---

### THE PROSPECT IS QUALIFIED WHEN:

There's enough fit

There's enough motivation

There's enough relationship

---

And that runs against the grain of what salespeople are taught (and often think/are paid) to do. Aren't you paid to pursue prospects until they either become customers or tell you to kiss off? Plus how do you know when it's time to stop pursuing a prospect? Many of you have had situations where a customer took forever, seemed to be playing you . . . then bought. So what's up with this "breaking up" stuff?

There are at least five reasons salespeople are loathe to cut a prospect loose.

**Reason #1: It's hard to disqualify prospects.** For instance, you simply may not know enough about them to accurately say whether they're truly qualified. More common, though, is our tendency to overestimate our prospects. You're sure there's a great fit. At least *you* see it. You're certain the prospect is motivated. At least *they* keep telling you how interested they are. You're convinced there's enough relationship. They're telling you they're the decision maker.

"We would be great together. She's told me how much she likes me. She makes her own decisions." Uh-huh.

**Reason #2: Sellers are trained to pursue deals to the death.** Most of you will keep that opportunity open in your CRM until it either turns into a deal or dies of old age. Until you hear a definite no or yes from the customer, you're gonna keep following up. Maybe less frequently over time, but you're still following up.

"So you're saying there's still a chance . . ."

**Reason #3: Sellers can't stand to lose.** You can tell by the millions of words worth of sales literature devoted to "overcoming objections" and "turning 'No' into 'Yes'" and exhortations of that sort. All those words are written by people who see "no deal" as a failure and don't like to lose.

"What do you mean we're breaking up? No, we're not."

**Reason #4: Insufficient pipeline.** If you don't have enough opportunities, and deadlines are coming up, everyone starts to look qualified. You need someone to follow up with, and they'll do.

See "sales goggles."

**Reason #5: Sellers believe they're paid to pursue prospects.** Your sales pipeline is most likely articulated as a set of sales stages that depict what you, the seller, do. Your sales manager looks at a stalled opportunity and asks you about what you've done to move it along. If you've done everything they can think of, and it's still not moving, the typical advice is to "move it to B level," which typically means continuing to pursue the prospect, only slightly less often.

"Hi, it's me again. Sorry I missed you again. I guess I'll try back later." (This is okay the first few times. This gets progressively less okay with repetition.)

## Reminder: What Sellers Are NOT Paid to Do

- pursue people until they get fed up with you or kick you out

- continue to follow up no matter what the response is

- keep prospects in your funnel until they buy or die of old age

What this really means: if you're not getting commitment, it might be time to move on.

But how do you know?

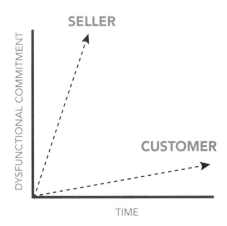

## Key Measurement: The Commitment Gap

It's tempting to say that if the customer isn't committing enough, soon enough, it's time to break up. That's often true, but sometimes low levels of commitment are just fine, as are slowly ascending levels of commitment. Sometimes you need to let conditions develop and opportunities germinate. Too much of a gap, though, and you have dysfunction, or lopsidedness, in the relationship. (Or you don't *have* a relationship.)

Sometimes taking it slow is best for both of you. You're both busy. Spend some time in the friend zone getting to know one another. Raise your hand if you know someone who should have taken this approach.[48]

---

48. It was really tempting to use the word germinate here too, but I made myself feel uncomfortable.

No, the key measurement here is the *difference* between your commitment and the customer's commitment—the gap between what each of you is putting into the relationship.[49]

I'll make it simple. If you experience, but don't address, a significant *commitment gap*, you are in for some undesirable consequences, both in business and in love, as in the following:

**Sales:** If you are selling but the customer isn't buying, you're not actually selling anything, are you? You have lots of dormant opportunities in your pipeline, and they clutter up your day. Your forecast is not an accurate prediction of what you will sell. Every minute you spend pursuing a non-opportunity reduces the time you have to spend on real opportunities. Your brand suffers from an unlimited supply of free follow-up. You don't seem like a busy, productive seller who people want to do business with.

**Love:** If you're dating someone and they aren't dating you back, you're not dating—you're stalking. Your little black book is full of useless entries, and looking at it makes you depressed. Your weekend plans are just weekend dreams. Every minute you spend stalking that movie star, you aren't spending finding the one for you. You look needy and desperate. You have a giant *L* on your forehead. For *Loser*.

So how do you know when it's time to break it off? That's like asking, "How do you know when the relationship is over?" There is no formula, only a set of interdependent factors:

- how many other opportunities you have

---

49. If the customer's commitment is outpacing yours, you have a service or delivery issue. That's another subject for another book.

- how good your other opportunities are

- your appetite for punishment and suffering

Was that cynical and jaded of me? Remember, we're talking about tough stuff here. There's a gap between what you're putting into the relationship, sales or love, and what you're getting back.

## Keys for Assessing the Commitment Gap

- **Look at trends, not the one-off.** Just because they stood you up for a meeting/date doesn't mean you're through. Too many of those in a row, though, and it might.

- **Use your common sense.** If it doesn't look or feel right, it often isn't. The problem is, salespeople are often under pressure that suppresses their common sense. True story: I once had a customer who promised me a bunch of work if I just proved myself through a pilot workshop. Oh, and was it okay if I gave them several extra blank workbooks? And if they had someone sit in the back of my pilot and "take notes"? I had a feeling I was walking into downtown Plagiarism City, but I was new to the business, and I didn't have enough clients. I got . . . sales goggles.

- **Ask your friends.** Isn't it funny how they always seem to see it before you do? Are we talking about sales or love here? Yes, we are.

- **Ask yourself, "Is there someplace better I could be?"** If the answer is yes, go there.

## How to Do It

Of course, it's easy to talk about dumping a prospect, but it's hard to do. We don't want to! There still might be a chance! We might be wrong, and they secretly want to buy; it's just not time yet!

Handled well, a good breakup call or e-mail (your choice) can address all these concerns:

- **Express regret**. After all, you are sorry to see that things aren't moving forward. You're calling out the commitment gap, but with regret (either real or manufactured).

- **Be clear.** Explain what your relationship will look like going forward. If you're going to stop calling them, tell them so. Don't tease them or lead them on.

- **Offer the possibility that you might have misunderstood their baffling lack of response or coldhearted attempts to use you.** Maybe you have misread the signs.

- **Leave the door open.** If they ever change their mind, you are here to serve them. In a sales sense, of course.

At this point you should be able to supply your own Lens of Love interpretation, yes?

## Why It Works

First of all, the breakup strategy works when it's real. You're not trying to trick them; you're calling out an authentic commitment gap. Do not use this strategy for evil!

Second, it works because of the law of supply and demand. When there is an unlimited, free supply of your follow-up or commitment, customers are less motivated to reciprocate. After all, why should I call you back if you're going to call me again, anyway? (Right now, you're thinking about the Lens of Love. You can't help it.) Conversely, it's amazing how often threatening to withdraw supply only serves to increase demand. The fact that you are unattainable makes me want you more.[50]

Ultimately, appropriate use of the breakup is important if you're going to avoid unhealthy, dysfunctional relationships and focus on reciprocal commitments that lead to long-lasting value.

## Suck Less at Selling:

- You are not paid to sell. You are paid to get commitment.

- Constantly assess commitment gaps.

- Ask yourself, "Is there someplace better I could be?"

- Have someplace better you could be. Nothing beats a full pipeline.

- Break up with class. Leave the door open.

---

50. Hypothetically speaking, that is.

# *Dumped with Dignity*

When I was a young seller, I once had a customer—a really good customer. They were everything I wanted in a customer—decision maker, budget, needs, you name it. They were the one for me. We did everything together—lunch, golf, dinner, drinks. They got great service and support from me, and I was their sole-source provider. The solutions worked. We just clicked.

So you can imagine my excitement as contract renewal time drew near. What an opportunity to take our relationship to the next level! How proud my sales manager would be when I brought home a contract with new services included, at increased margins!

Yes, of course, other vendors pursued this customer, offering inducements, but I had the inside track. I was the incumbent! Nonetheless, I remained attentive—business reviews, needs assessment, meeting more of the team, introducing my executives, the works. I left no stone unturned in my desire to lock down the business. How excited I was to increase the depth and breadth of our relationship.

Then, one day, the phone rang. It was the customer.

"Dan," she said, "I'm sorry to say, I'm not going to be able to renew with you. You know I love working with you, and you've provided a ton of value. It's just that we feel your competition is simply a better fit for what we need right now, and we've chosen another vendor.

"I certainly appreciate what you've done for me," she continued. "But we feel this is the best move for the business. Trust me. It was nothing you did wrong. If anything changes in the future, I'll be sure to let you know. Thanks again."

Do I even need to lay it out? Didn't you already go there in your mind? Tough beans. I'm doing it anyway. You're going steady. You're great together. You have fun and share the same interests. Her parents love you. Your families have met. Everything just clicks. You can't wait for the prom. Then the phone rings. "Dan," she says, "I'm sorry, but I'm breaking up with you.[51] I like Tony better, and I'm going to the prom with him. You're a really sweet guy. It's not you; it's me. I hope we can still be friends."

**Business reaction:** Whaaaaaat???

**Lens of Love reaction:** Whaaaaaaaaaaaaaaaaaaaaaaaaaaat?!?!?!?!?!

## The Sales Reaction

This is another of those scenarios I typically lay in front of my sales training workshop participants (customized for your industry, of course!), followed by this question:

How would you respond?

Well, how would *you* respond? How many of these boxes would you check if your best customer just dumped you?

---

51. Hypothetical example. This has never happened to me.

❏ I would call the customer back immediately.

❏ I would ask the customer why they chose somebody else.

❏ I would ask the customer what happened—what did I miss?

❏ I would ask the customer to define "We've chosen . . ." Have they signed a purchase order?

❏ I would ask the customer what I could do to win back the business.

❏ I would tell the customer why I think they should stick with my company.

❏ I would tell the customer about the risks and costs of going with a new vendor.

❏ I would warn the customer about the weaknesses of the solution they chose.

❏ I would have my manager/boss call the customer to see what could be done.

❏ I would call the customer's peers to see if they could change my customer's mind.

❏ I would call the customer's boss in an attempt to postpone/reverse the decision.

How'd you do? Admit it, you checked more than one box . . . and you thought about checking more. It's okay—these are natural reactions, some of which you may be required to perform.

These also happen to be the reaction of . . . someone who just got dumped! A scorned lover!

You know we have to look at these through the Lens of Love—it's just too juicy! For variety and laughs, let's quote a typical scorned lover (dumpee) on the phone with the person who just dumped them (dumper). As we go along, why don't you check the boxes of the tactics you would employ in love.

- ❏ "Hey, it's me. I just got your call. Can we talk?"
- ❏ "Why are you breaking up with me? Why would you choose Tony over me?"
- ❏ "What happened? What went wrong? What did I miss?"
- ❏ "What do you mean you've decided? Has he bought you a wrist corsage yet?"
- ❏ "What do I have to do to win you back?"
- ❏ "You should go to the prom with me instead. I can show you a much better time."
- ❏ "Tony doesn't know you like I know you. He doesn't appreciate you like I do."
- ❏ "Tony is a loser. He's just using you. He picks his nose and eats the boogers."
- ❏ "Hello, Lisa? This is Dan's mom . . . "
- ❏ "Would you please tell your friend Lisa that she's making a big mistake?"
- ❏ "Hello, Lisa's mom? Did you know who your daughter's about to go to the prom with? You've got to stop her!"

Here's my scoring system, for both the business version and the love version:

0–3 boxes checked: You're a scorned seller/lover, and you can be expected to react that way. Not great, though.

3–6 boxes checked: You're desperate, probably because your pipeline/dating possibilities are limited.

6–11 boxes checked: Creepy! Stalker alert!

## I Smell What You're Stepping In

Again, I understand that you may be under pressure from management/your parents to employ some of these tactics. Most salespeople in my workshops say they would be in trouble if they *didn't* do something. But before you take rash (and potentially brand-damaging) action, stop and ask yourself these questions:

1. Is the customer looking forward to your call? Are they hoping you call them back?

    - If not, you may want to reconsider that move entirely.

    - If you're required to do so anyway, okay. Good luck.

2. How do you want to be perceived?

    - The choices: dignified second-place finisher, undignified loser, creepy loser.

3. What's your long-term strategy?

    - Is this the only shot you have?

- Or will you be around the next day and the day after?

- What's your time horizon?

4. How desperate are you?

- If the answer is *super desperate*, you are going to check these boxes.

- If you have enough prospects (in business or in love), you will employ fewer or none of the tactics listed above.

For the nondesperate, the dignified, and those wishing to appear that way, here is my suggestion.

## Take the High Road

- Send a congratulatory note right away. Period.

- Express disappointment and regret. Do not accompany with begging.

- Let some time pass. The more jilted you feel, the more you need to pause.

- After a pause, ask for the lesson. Do not accompany with an offer to change unless desperate or required to do so. For example, a lower-price offer in this situation has negative consequences in terms of margins/profit that make at least one of you regret the deal later.

- Help them be successful.

- Offer to be there when they're ready. Again, this depends on your time horizon and your long-term strategy.

- Wait for them to realize the error of their ways. (The other vendor overpromised! Tony is a convicted felon and a recidivist!)

- Be there to pick up the pieces when it's time. No-pressure, periodic touches ensure you're there when the timing is right.

- Avoid the "I told you so." Everyone knows. Saying so out loud is for your needs, not theirs. Besides, it's undignified.

Let's face it: getting dumped sucks—in business and in love (not that I'd know about the latter, of course). These techniques do not change the reasons *why* you got dumped. I've dealt with those throughout this book. The high road is purely about *how* you handle it. Get dumped with dignity.

## Suck Less at Selling:

- Choose the dignified response, in selling and in love.

- That is all.

# Conclusion
## Love Is All You (Really) Need

It's time to take off the heart-shaped glasses. I think you get it by now.

Relationship sellers, my fondest wish for you is that the Lens of Love becomes an internal filter you use to evaluate your strategies, tactics, and behaviors. How you view the world (your confirmation bias) influences your behavior. I want the Lens of Love to be part of your bias—a bias toward behaviors that would work just as well in courtship as they would in selling.

When you look through the Lens, business opportunities are the result of the relationship, not just the point of the relationship. Your focus is on the person with needs, not just the business with needs. Problems represent opportunities to help, not just transactions to be won. And selling becomes a true relationship (people who feel attached to each other) and not just a business relationship (providing a product or service).

This core focus on true relationships will matter *more* as advancing technologies increase the speed of business. For example, as I write this, 3-D printers are transforming manufacturing. Today, engineers can scan a competitor's product, print a replica, and produce their own version in a matter of days, not months. The window of competitive advantage is so small now as to give product managers ulcers. Even in 3-D printing, expiring patents have spawned a legion of new, low-cost entrants into the market.

And let's face it. You very likely already have competitors whose solutions are more or less indistinguishable to the unsophisticated customer. Competing (and sometimes specious) claims from marketers begin to mirror each other so closely that only the logos (or mascots, etc.) stand out.

What also remain when you strip your product/service differentiation away are people, their needs, and their feelings. You will win, and continue to win, if you're the best at understanding your customers as people, helping them meet their needs, and respecting their feelings.

It is that simple, and it's nothing new. Throughout history, we humans have run our affairs from the heart first (or the emotional, limbic brain, technical people), the head second.

Sell like you love, and you develop relationships that stand the test of time and competition.

Love is the answer. Let love rule.

Love,
Dan

# Acknowledgements

Warren Wechsler, thanks for showing me through your example that this career existed. The epiphany I had that day in your workshop changed the course of my professional life.

Tom Piechura, thanks for beating me out for that sales management job at the Daily, then hiring me to work with you. You taught me about competing, then cooperating as professionals. And about losing to someone better qualified for the job.

Rich Meiss, thanks for helping me understand the business I'm in today, and for believing in my ability to succeed in this business, even before others did. Also, you're one of the world's nicest humans ever.

Lynn Solem, thanks for showing me how a consummate professional conducts business in the face of brutal travel, demanding clients, and challenging work. You taught me how to bring myself to the work. Rest in peace.

Mary Jo Ready, thanks for the great partnership. I enjoyed being your clients' virtual sales training department for all those years, and you were a treat to work with. And very patient.

Brad Maendler, Brad Guck, Carolyn Herfurth, Jeff Wendorf, Steve Krebsbach, and the rest of the crew I spent time with in Sparkslandia, thanks for the companionship and camaraderie. You taught me about the value of good coworkers . . . and quality leads.

Matt McDarby, Michele White, Mary Casper, Phil Knowles, James Dean, Ed Albertson, Stephanie Woods, and the rest of the HINC crew, thanks for the steady flow of well-organized work with cool clients. I got a real-world education in world-class selling through our engagements.

Gregg Hodges, thanks for the opportunity to get into the lab and test my theories on sales management. From you I learned about the value of the COO perspective in managing sales organizations, and how speed is good.

Brian Kibby and Cindy Sullivan, thanks for the most fun and the most fundamental impact I've ever had at work. From you I learned the value of talent, culture, and strategy, in that order.

Erin McGinty, thanks for the opportunity to know you and learn about love through you. From you I learned what is possible, and that life is too short and too precious. Rest in peace.

Jacob and Erin, thanks for being excellent children and a joy in my life. I've received so much more from you than I could ever give back. I'm looking forward to seeing what wonderful humans you turn out to be. I love you.

Donna Boatman, thanks for being my spouse of twenty years, my best friend, the mother of my children, and my partner through many of life's important changes. With you I've learned about what love can be. Thank you.

Mom and Dad, thanks for adopting me and giving me every opportunity to succeed. From you I learned sacrifice and unconditional love—if it was conditional on behavior, I would have been fired.

Hanna Kjeldbjerg and the rest of the crew at Beaver's Pond Press, thanks for your expertise, keen eyes, and excellent project management. This book is much better because of you.

Shannon Taylor, thanks for helping me get this book started. From you I learned the discipline of writing . . . and the power of the word count.

To my former clients and lovers, thanks for letting me learn on your time. And I'm sorry for not having learned it all sooner.

To you, thanks for reading. I love you too.

# *Recommended Reading List*

Have you ever read one of those comprehensive, technically accurate bibliographies where the authors and publishers and all that are listed out? Me neither.

Here are three reasons I could not care less about a bibliography:

1. I didn't cite enough books to make a legitimate bibliography. That would require research. This is not a research paper, this is an essay.

2. Making an actual bibliography is so boring: I couldn't even find someone to pay to do it.

3. You don't care. You're going to Google the title. Done.

So the heck with that—no bibliography! I'm not even putting these in alphabetical order! I'm not even underlining them! AUTHOR OUT OF CONTROL!

**The Five Love Languages** (Gary Chapman)—About the different ways we give and prefer love and how to speak each other's languages. **Spoiler alert:** Everyone is different.

**Why Marriages Succeed and Fail** (John Gottman)—About the factors that make or break loving relationships, based on some incredible research. **Spoiler alert:** Contempt and resentment will kill you.

**Crucial Confrontations** (Kerry Patterson, Joseph Grenny, Ron McMillan, and Al Switzler)—About mastering the skills necessary to have the candid conversations that matter in loving relationships. **Spoiler alert:** It's about mastering yourself first.

**Blink** (Malcolm Gladwell)—About the power of thin-slicing (making judgments based on super-limited info) and how that helps and hurts us. **Spoiler alert:** In selling, thin-slicing works both better and worse than we think it does.

**Getting to Yes** (Roger Fisher and William Ury)—About negotiating fairly without giving in. The grandfather of modern negotiating. **Spoiler alert:** Start with interests, not positions, and don't give in to tactics.

**The Goal** (Eliyahu Goldratt)—About managing to the constraints in any complex system. This book is like an MBA in manufacturing process. **Spoiler alert:** Manage the bottlenecks and you have managed the system.

**Antifragile** (Nassim Taleb)—About how to hedge against and profit from the impact of highly improbable events. **Spoiler alert:** It's all about options and enough small bets.

**The Long Tail** (Chris Anderson)—About how to capitalize on niche markets in a digital age. **Spoiler alert:** It's about scaling yourself.

**Unlimited Power** (Tony Robbins): About the power of NLP (neurolinguistic programming) to redirect both behaviors and attitude. **Spoiler alert:** It's all about having the right models to emulate.

**Traffic** (Tom Vanderbilt)—About behavioral psychology applied to the study of moving death machines. **Spoiler alert:** The safer we feel, the riskier we act.

**SPIN Selling** (Neil Rackham)—About using a questioning method to uncover customer needs and advance sales. **Spoiler alert:** Problems are the seed of the need, and questions are the gardener's tool.

**Mastering the Complex Sale** (Jeff Thull)—About managing the moving parts that must coalesce in a complex opportunity. **Spoiler alert:** It's about having the right people in the right places.

**The Seven Habits of Highly Effective People** (Stephen Covey)—About fundamental principles of life. **Spoiler alert:** It's all about what you control and what you do about that.

**Quiet** (Susan Cain) About our bias toward the extrovert and the underrated power of the introvert. **Spoiler alert**: Ambiverts make the best salespeople in complex, relationship sales.

# *Index*

Nope. No index either. What kind of a book do you think this is, anyway?

## *About ~~the Author~~ Me*

Dan Smaida consults with high-level sales organizations around the world to . . .

Do you dismiss sections like these because they're a bunch of self-aggrandizing hype? I sure do. BORING.

Instead, how about an "About the Author" with a little more reality to it? Here are eleven facts about me, ten of which I bet most business authors are not sharing.

- I still chew on my fingernails when under extreme stress.

- Although I mock them publicly, I enjoy bunnies. And kittens.

- Some days I forget to brush my teeth. Am I the only one who misses every so often?

- My Mount Rushmore of food includes the mighty Big Mac.

- I cry.

- My first band in high school was a Beach Boys cover band. We were almost awesome.

- My primary love languages are physical touch and words of appreciation.

- I like a clean countertop. In fact, I like all my horizontal surfaces uncluttered.

- I am a classic example of the saying, "You teach what you need to learn."

- In high school, my least favorite nickname was . . . you know, I'm not even going there. I don't want to get that crap started again.

- I have a lovely family, including two wonderful children, an assortment of mammals, and a tiny farm in the woods of Western Wisconsin where I consult, play music, and write. I'm a lucky dude.